AF471739

ON THE COVER

On the front cover is an original painting that I created several years ago. It is an interpretation of the culminating events of "Fixed Stars Rise." It is entitled "The Precession of the Equinoxes."

The drawings on the back cover are interpretations of the sequences of awareness in the evolution of consciousness, both individual and group. They are entitled "Birth," "Presentation," "Transformation," and "Renewal."

The images on both covers were photographed by Eric M. Vasquez.

FIXED STARS RISE

CHARLES T. LAFFODAY

MHP
muse house press

FIXED STARS RISE

CHARLES T. LAFFODAY

MHP
muse house press

MHP
muse house press

ISBN: 978-1-935827-03-0

Trade Paperback
© Copyright 2010 Charles T. Laffoday
All Rights reserved

Request for information and rights should be addressed to:
Muse House Press

Find us on the Internet at:
www.MuseHousePress.com

Muse House Press is an imprint of Muse House Press, Inc.

Cover Design: Donald Brennan / YakRider Media
Interior Composition: Donald Brennan / YakRider Media

Up to 10% of each chapter may be reproduced as quotes provided attribution to the author is made. Other use may only be made with written permission of the publisher or author.

Printed in the United States of America

DEDICATION

I would like to dedicate this book to the late, great Thomas A. Boyd, whose entire life was a celebration of theatrical extravagance.

ACKNOWLEDGMENTS

I want to thank Jerilyn Clayton Nash for her tireless support, assistance, unflinching open-mindedness, and constructive insight while editing the contents of this book.

I would like to thank everyone at Muse House Press for their encouragement and for helping me to get this work published.

I would like to thank Donald Brennan for his meticulousness, professionalism and respect for my whims and quirks while facilitating its publication.

PROLOGUE

A signal emerged from an egg, floating in chaos...and began to digress. It pondered the beginning, professing a theoretical gradualism, seeking an eventual grasp of an understanding. It would reach a place that would seem so close, only to see it fade. It would profess a theoretical punctualism, seeking to surprise it with bursts of inspiration. Again, it would get close, only to see it fade.

It was disregarded, relegated to memories, images scried in weightless pools. It was repressed, flickering in the corners as long-forgotten afterthoughts, resounding in the echoes of disappearing tongues. It was castigated, labeled as ugliness by a guise of honesty, masquerading beneath a shield of saintliness. Finally, it was abandoned and left to die, disowned by family, buried as a footnote in another's book of legacy.

Still, it searched. There were elements of space, composition and color. There was a developing allegory, a medium of afflatus in the mythology of design. It pursued the cycles of birth, presentation, transformation and renewal. Yet, it sought more...a deeper expression. Spirituality was unsatisfying. Religion was insulting. Dreams were misinterpreted.

Amidst a suggestion of an anecdote beside a photograph of a picture...was a familiar reference, a vehicle for reverie...

• • •

The minutes, hours and days passed for another period. He had an intuition that Night had just passed her cloak over his realm.

• • •

INTRODUCTION

The rule of Jove had ended. When he spoke to the heavens, the pantheon was supposed to listen. Most of them did. It was spoken with a brutal honesty: one that precluded the admittance of an error of his opinion. There was an official protocol: the aegis of his authority was set to the timbre of his voice; the jurisprudence of his counsel was meted out by his overwhelming presence. It was patriarchal and authoritative. It was also wise and deep-thinking. Sometimes, it was even kind-hearted. It had a strange, dictatorial zealousness for the enforcement of law, both just and unjust...dispensed through displaced emotion.

He was the protector. Some of them loved him for his clarity amidst conflicting messages. Some of them hated him for this compartmentalization. Almost all of them feared the reality of his force. Still, there was a compliance in this structure: Their positive social interaction was created from the threat of negative consequences. They could lie and cheat and steal, but eventually, they would have to face his wrath.

It was a peculiar freedom when he fell. They had grown so reliant upon his dictums that they lacked a sense of integrity, an ethical proprioception. Their individual morality was attached to that which they could do in lieu of him, concealed from him, or to gain his favor. Their collective morality was based upon a contingency: It must serve his glorification. When his authority ended, they turned on each other.

* *

It was said that Prometheus touched some of the creatures with an abundance of fluidity. It was they who first acquired the rudiments of civilization. It was they who began to disseminate the original sparks. It was they who spread the word.

They spread the word very well. They even created symbols of it so they could write it down. They embraced the word because they wanted to feel it. They were not so interested in elaborating upon it: They would celebrate the moment.

Their fluidity slowly seemed to work against them, however. The more structured ones had begun to embrace the word, too, but they made it more complex. They paid as much attention to the past and the future as they did to the present. The more fluid ones fell behind the more structured ones.

They had received many sparks, but theirs seemed to scatter into different directions, for unclear purposes. They became insecure. They came to believe that they lacked the sense of structure that is necessary to bring a creative notion to fruition. They began to feed off their emotions.

Prometheus touched some of the creatures with an abundance of structure. It was they who took the word and specialized it. It was they who began to constrict the original sparks. It was they who focused upon the word.

They focused upon the word very well. They made it so efficient that it became institutionalized. They embraced the word because they wanted to bring order to it. They were not so interested in expressing it: They would celebrate a sense of place.

Their structure slowly seemed to work against them, however. They were awed by the fruits of the creative realms: They wanted their own voice. They studied the originals; then, they made their own versions. Still, they did not satisfy.

Something vital was missing: They had effectively learned to copy.

They had received many sparks, but theirs seemed to be too forced, too mechanical. They became insecure. They came to believe that they lacked the creative abilities that are necessary to vivify a realized notion. They began to grow rigid.

Prometheus touched some of the creatures with comparatively equal amounts of fluidity and structure. It was they who took the word and nuanced it. It was they who realized the word.

They realized the word very well. They embellished it so that things and experiences could no longer be described by one symbol: A color had many shapes and hues. They even created laws to protect the pursuit of such subtleties: They would celebrate the creative process.

Their parity slowly seemed to work against them, however. They were criticized by the other groups as being arrogant for possessing this comparative position of balance. The more fluid group said that they did not show enough passion. The more structured group said that they should be more serious. They tried to be more like the others... They began to immerse themselves in fluidity, but soon began to drown. Then, they attempted to reestablish themselves within the confines of structure, only to forget the joy of the creative process.

They had received many sparks, but theirs seemed not to penetrate the essence of a thing. They became insecure. They came to believe that they lacked the ability to stress varying aspects of a notion enough to ever truly understand the whole. They began to lose balance.

• • •

I still love you, my Dears. Our bond has grown unique through the ages...like staged foreplay for a distant lover's affection.

Well, a note to all: Previous applicants need not apply!

• • •

CHAPTER ONE

An image appears in the reaches of the heavens. It is no phantasm. It is substantive. It has gained forward motion. It has not yet been noticed, but it is not disguised. Saturn is moving and increasing his speed: He is leaving his low points behind.

It seemed as if he were rolling along with life... and then he ran into them. At least, he remembers hitting what he thought was one. Then, he would hit a newer and deeper one. He remembers feeling devalued, like unheeded emotion. It lingered as a chant, a pang from a distance.

It had seemed that their energies were made for each other. Prometheus was more active in the beginning, and more passive in the end. He, himself, was more passive in the beginning and more active in the end.

He had been searching for such a sacred cycle. Instead, he had found this strange oracle. He had come to believe that it was also deceptive. He had returned to it seeking answers, but the questions came from someplace else. He felt alone at a tainted wellspring.

There was a dullness. There was a numbness. He began to lose the ability to focus deeply for long periods of time. Then, he lost the ability to focus deeply. Soon, he could not focus at all.

The pain left his heart and travelled about his body. It moved slowly, but it was curious of all points. It reached expression in unexpected ways, like a mutation of a manufactured virus...one step ahead, while leaving no prints. It kept coming. It stayed longer than he had wanted to imagine: He had to seek help.

He searched for a healer, but could only find a specialist. This specialist could not cure him, however. He told him that his problem did not fall into his area of specialization. He asked the specialist if he could help him with his pain. The specialist told him that it was important to be numb to a patient's pain. He could better serve the patient if he were numb to his pain. He would, however, arrange for another specialist to see him. It would take only several weeks to make an appointment.

This specialist could not cure him. He was specialized too, but not in that area. He asked this specialist if he could help him with his pain. This specialist told him that he knew the previous specialist, and had great respect for him. They were colleagues. They belonged to a fraternity of specialists. He would not have made any mistakes. He could, however, arrange for another specialist to see him. It would take several more weeks to make an appointment.

This one, too, could not find a cure. He grew tired. He felt lost. He could not even locate his legend. Still, it seemed as if he were going to pieces. His sense of time seemed altered. He knew that he remained in these exiled territories, yet he felt ensnared in a lexical maze by a conspiracy of jargon from the pages of a mission statement.

The minutes, hours and days passed for another period. He had an intuition that Night had just passed her cloak over his realm. Then, an instinct led him to look into his timepiece, which was catching the light of a luminous body. He saw a face. He saw his reflection. It glowed as a strange, pale, lustration.

He had reached this place that he had not wanted to see: It lay in a deep state of empathy. Somehow, he felt unconsciously drawn to it with every step. He had reached this place, and he felt a fulfillment of an imperative to heed an esoteric call, embedded in an instinct.

Soon, he saw an image surrounded by sickness. This image was spinning like a roomful of vortices, mounted on the ceiling and reflected in a window. He was picked up by this motion. It was unlike anything that he had known. His entire being was in shock. He had never known such a fulguration.

He viewed scenes of impressive rock mountains. He was moving. He was searching. He flew over them, looking for inspiration. Still, they were brown and self-contained, early deposits frozen in time. They were dry, negative places, stones in a cactus garden, monoliths of toxicity.

Next, he viewed scenes of expansive forests. The view from afar resembled trees and other life forms. He hiked inside them. He was attracted to the turgor of green, the color of nature. A closer look, however, revealed a caustic hue, a chemical process. He approached them and found only stands of toxicity.

He viewed scenes of vast seas. He swam underneath them. The rocks below had facades of chiseled faces. Quiet trams snaked with an absence of tourists. Pockets of water magnified the surroundings. There were teeming reefs of yellow and schools of silvery objects, disjecta from an unknown vessel. They fluttered and were dispersed by a wave, unsettled refuses of toxicity.

Then, everything shifted, like a blow to the head, a forthright charge into invisible impediments. It pulled him down to where the broken spirit hides, dwelling among life's painful events and unrealized dreams, searching for a renewal in a past obscured by honed absurdities, densely packed, until there is only one way to sort it all out.

****

"It is like an anesthesia...the more one sleeps...the more quickly one awakes..."

A hand caresses a material.

"How do you like it? I had only one request: It should be the perfect frame for our context: festively modern yet fabulously retro. It is a reinterpretation of a number that I wore...immortalized one night in ancient Etruria---that land so dear...where every valiant pursuit was measured solely by its capacity to increase the enjoyment of life, or to savor its importance---by a hircine sculpture with piercing, olive eyes, impossibly thick calves and large, proletarian hands...which he couldn't keep off of me.

It was a celebration in honor of Bacchus inside a massive, hilltop temple that was being consecrated to his devotion. The revelers arrived all day and all night, each choosing an appropriate entrance. The entrance on the left was signified by a painting of a heterosexual couple having sex...adjacent to an image of a bereft, dispirited bull. The entrance on the right was signified by a painting of a male homosexual couple having sex adjacent to an image of a lively, spirited bull.

It shall be duly noted that inside this entrance on the right, amidst throngs of naked, muscled Tarquinian youths flexing and dancing in open cages to the sounds of lyres and flutes...this intense young artist taught me the mysteries of the Disciplina Etrusca. It was a spectacle whose only remaining traces can be found in art history books, and a handful of museums. Strangely, these boots are every bit as tight as the ones that I wore on that night...but when we emerged the next day, I was uncannily attuned to the rhythms of the songs of the cicadas, the patterns in the air of formicating no-seeums, the fickle territoriality of owls to the domiciles of certain persons and the breath-like mussitations of summer lightning along the horizon. Still, the strangest fact of all is that those uncomfortable boots were the only things that I was wearing.

The following day, we hiked deep into the Appenines so that at night we could stare at the stars. It was there that he swore his undying devotion to me... Admittedly, I was impressed with his strength of conviction, so I secured from him his date of birth, from which I could draw his natal horoscope to surmise our compatibility. It was then that I realized that only his ascendant was in my quadruplicity, as I had suspected all along.

Forthrightly, I could feel the walls of possessiveness encircling me like the joined hands of former lovers. My senses were overwhelmed with an image of the tines of a fork repeatedly trying to pierce a sweet, green pea...which just as consistently rolled out from under its tines. Still, only one thing remained unclear to me: I couldn't tell if I were the fork or if I were the pea... In any event, I excused myself to answer a call of nature, and I never saw him again.

An eye is cast into the audience.

"I still love you, my Dears. Our bond has grown unique through the ages...like staged foreplay for a distant lover's affection. Well, a note to all: Previous applicants need not apply!"

A pose is absconded after sufficient acknowledgement.

"I suppose that we need a universal frame of reference. Let's begin from the beginning, so to speak...these queens...these queens!"

Mercury clears his throat. A strong aroma of something that smells like a fine coffee escapes with his breath.

"In any case, I surmise that the most pertinent aspects of this story began when Prometheus and Saturn renewed their acquaintance after what I have been told had seemed like forever. In fact, none of us was there. At least, we were not aware of what was happening. I cannot, therefore, be as accurate with my statements as our subscribers have come to expect. Still, our words shall not be like those of our many recent competitors: parceled out and partisan to the handful of monopolies that own them. Ours are the last words, the official words, the most respected words in the business. Our sources have been verified with an impeccable accuracy. We shall recount, rather than recant: Ours is the voice of the ubiquitous grapevine!"

Illustrations glow behind him in order of importance. Occasionally, he will take his scepter and point to one for the purpose of clarification. It is a delivery that is supposed to promote intimacy with the viewer. Somehow, however, he seems a little like a piano teacher who might like to rest his hands upon those of his struggling student, while sitting very close. His exhalation produces an aroma that is reminiscent of a fine coffee, mixed with a sweet mint.

"Dear, I have been sitting on the vapors of previously unreleased material...Mefitis! Mefitis! Let me catch my breath..."

He remembers a list of etiquette that he read at a dusty shelf in a vintage store: Take a moment to check body language; high-status is conveyed by holding eye-contact; a confident pose can be quite effective, too; a body must not be tense; emphasize important words and articulate well; project, but do not shout; try to breathe from the diaphragm.

"In any case, Saturn was in exile from the environs of Earth. Many ages had passed since his last acts of authority on most of her ground. His son, Jupiter, the 'great benefic,'" he states, as he clears his throat and rolls his eyes, "had become the ruler of the pantheon on Olympus.

"Oh, I say 'his son, Jupiter,' and this fact is true, but in reality Saturn never actually sired his supposed children. This conception was the result of a miraculous sleight of hand—or sleight of something—by Rhea. He certainly never touched her in the morning, evening or afternoon. Dear, that story goes something like 'And a fertile rain fell..."

He clears his throat again.

"In any case, Jupiter had overthrown Saturn. Now, I am quite aware that these documented events are quite well-known, but an overview is an essential part of the historical record. Still, redundancies have as much appeal to me as chopped phrases and overworn expressions. Ergo, I promise that I shall strive to stick to the pith of the story – the unadulterated pith.

"In any case..."

Clio looks at him, but remains too quiet. She is smiling, but her teeth look precariously clenched, like white icing roses on the edge of a cake, untouched and forever embalmed under crystal display. She is sipping on a highball in a deep glass, with no ice. It is concealed as a citrus-based purification drink.

He rethinks his wording.

"Jupiter had become the administer of the heavens, and much of Earth. The jurisprudence of this pantheon was in his hands—or at least his control—over almost all of these realms.

"Dear, the heavens moved; yet, he would not surrender his rule. More than nine signs in the precession of the equinoxes passed; yet, he would not surrender his rule.

"Saturn, however, before his exile, had taken a final refuge in a land that escaped Jove's purview, in what is now Italy. Stories of the peace and prosperity of his scaled-down reign there are quite well-known. It must be noted that this late rule of Saturn's was known to be a golden one—and, Dear, I know the difference between a thing that is gilded, and a thing that is golden."

At this moment, he pulls on his right earlobe. He pulls on it until Clio notices his tasteful earring...his most recent acquisition. He pulls on it until she gets a good look at it. It was derived from a very rich vein.

"Jupiter could not allow his father's influence to threaten his rule. Dear, he actually believed that the worlds revolved around him. He—and others in our pantheon—joined forces against Saturn again. This time they proceeded to boot him from the peninsula of Italy, and expel him to the outermost reaches of the heavens.

"It was a busy 'home away from home.' It seems that every wayfarer has a close-encounter to tell... Of course, such rumor-mills produce the excelsior of legend. Tales are told and yarns are spun... Trade-papers reported the most recent sightings, competing for coverage of far-away flings. Documentaries were made from unofficial outtakes... Sentences were stopped before they were finished. Words were purposely removed from their context. Pictures were taken were no one was invited..."

Painted eyebrows trace a high, unlikely arc.

"Dear, I intend to separate the furbelow from the frock!

"Of course, his dear love, Prometheus, had a role to play in all of this. I told him not to trust him. I reminded him that I have had lots of experience in these matters, but he would not listen. Prometheus knew just what to do: He sought the company of Jove. He told him that he admired his cunning. He said that it was a new era...one where cunning would prevail. He encouraged him to rise-up against his fellow Titans. He even took up arms: He turned on him. It was his assistance that enabled Jove to succeed. He was the instigator of the Titanomachy.

* *

A message was passed on the lips of the prodigal sons as a celestial stage was being prepared in an enveloping borealis of the colors of the spectrum. Gifts were arriving in colorful wrappings of streamline modernism... Symbols of penises were festooned in a multitude of finery from every cultural tradition. The most muscular of the magi were dancing shirtless to this theme at all-night parties.

Concomitantly, a social constraint was composed: This advent shall be officially banned. Then, it shall be framed in a reference to its deepest restrictions, notions inculcated into the earliest memories like artifacts lying under layers of dirt. They were said to be sacred and shrouded in mystery, undefined, yet present...nude figures mixing from separate steam-rooms. Taboos were created to protect its sanctity. It was said to be the means of the workings of the universe, theoretical dynamics of masculine and feminine energy.

It was said to be electric: a charge between two points. The way of the current is to follow the urge, moving from high to low in areas of potential...following a path of least resistance. It was said to be magnetic: a field of lines of force that get stronger near a conductor...also seeking a path of least resistance, while entering and exiting at magnetic poles. It was a system that was based upon inherent polarization.

This realization seduced him into a distant state where he felt less cautious than usual. He felt a strange kind of wanderlust. He had an urge to explore an old tale of wonder... He visited this world which—although unmapped—lies in a realm that is empathic, yet somehow ambivalent. He went to this place that offers up mysteries.

Its atmosphere was mood-lit, as he fell into a romantic daze. He awoke at a place of an oracle, to the sight of another. He didn't recognize him at first; he didn't recognize him at all. The attraction was undeniable: It came from the gut. His senses were heightened... There was an emotional stimulation where the excesses of embellishment are laid-bare, or brought forth. The strands of their energies wrapped-up into each other almost immediately. He felt like a Lesbian.

He walked the grounds of the planet, thinking of him. All of this world seemed to remind him of him. He saw messages of symbolism in a synchronous terrain. There, in the sky, was a philosopher's model...a circle in a circle, a halo around a satellite, an image of the micro repeated in the macro. It was a psychological study, like the opposite side of a familiar coin, or a meeting in the middle of an ersatz priapus.

He introduced himself, and they began to talk. They sensed a familiarity that still stands at a distance. Slowly, they stood closer...and closer still. It was the smell of his neck, the pressing of his touch. It was as it had always been, a reliquary that had not lost its shrine; it had maintained its beauty, and could not be exploited. It was like an extended song fragment, waiting for its realization. It took him back...

The worlds were new. The energies were raw. They were very young, but they were already themselves. They were not the only ones, but they were among the first. They felt a little different from most of the others: They were already apparent. Outside was intolerance, but their shelter was strong. They had made a perfect place in a circle of trees. There were arbors of berries under heavenly bamboo...lush when natural, yet, beautiful when dried for effect in display.

It was as it had always been...as they had always known. They had found each other, and they had fallen in love. Soon, they found a way to consecrate their bond. No one ever told them, but they knew what to do. They knew each other better than anyone else.

He rolled over on top of him.

"Tell me if you want me to stop."

"Okay."

"Okay...you want me to stop?"

"Okay............I'll let you know!"

He loved to look into Prometheus' eyes. They were the best thing of all. He felt a place for himself there... He could see a look of admiration. He could see a look of desire. He could see a look of belonging. He could see a look of relief. It certainly looked like home to him.

Somehow, he recognized this one... What a bounty he had found! He was no stranger to the delights of variety, but it seemed different with Prometheus. It seemed different and he could feel it. He could even smell it, a virile whiff on a scheming frame. It induced an altered state, preternatural...strong but fresh, like the first scent of sweat detected from an athlete, just after he has bathed.

Prometheus would come alive when he would show him attention. He was a slinking cheetah in an open field, a growling cat on top of his totem: Every egomaniac knows what to do with a letter of acclaim. He loved to be chased more than anything, though it wasn't like it as with the others: He knew that he was worthy of it. He required adoration, and he lived to be pursued. He especially loved it when he, Saturn, was the pursuer. He felt like a "Diana" on the trail of a "trophy stag," a sacred hunt where every scented leaf and branch was tagged for reverence.

It was really getting to him. He even read romantic poetry. He read and recited and felt the words of wings and clippings and cages and ecstasy. Things only got worse: He began to listen to romantic songs. He heard and sang and felt the sounds of the notes and chords and souls and reunions. It was embarrassing. There was a dirty little bathos that could not be expunged, even by its caricature.

* *

Mercury clears his throat. He shall not refrain from most prerequisites of clear and precise speech. Still, he loves the "new" journalism. He adores the use of inflections. He has a tendency to stress the first noun or adjective of each sentence. He can be a little fussy, but he should never, never be accused of being abecedarian. His words might seem slightly forced: They are accompanied by a pained but unsurprised tone of artistic boredom.

"Meanwhile, the years that were passing saw many changes on Earth, and in the heavens. These changes came rapidly, and often with no clear and instructive purpose. Hmmm…throw a coin in the air and see where it lands, Dear.

"The age of WHAT?"

Clio takes a moment to absorb the cynical energy. It is renewing, allowing her to maintain her focus. She is not quite happy unless she or someone else is talking about how "bad" things are. She acknowledges him with a finessed sound of caution from high in the palate, an effective deterrent to the contraindications of expediency.

Once again, he has strayed from the basics: Reports should be filed in a linear fashion; everything begins with the cultivation of sources; be available and ask direct questions; do not be afraid to ask them more than once; make a personal interest of gathering details; try to keep it strictly on the record; construct an outline before beginning; be specific! Never develop a friendship with a source.

They will need more information: A newsworthy topic requires a catchy headline; write down ideas in the margins of transcripts; facts and details have to be checked; reference books should be located next to the desk; grasp the essence of what is to be said; wordiness is an obstacle that is best avoided. Always remember to ask this question: Can it be more concise?

She is a busy professional, and she loves her job. Her hair is perhaps a little too long, but still quite practical. She likes to flip it back—just behind the shoulder—on both sides, when she walks down a hallway. Of course, she prefers a shoe with an established heel. There is not a more respected authority on history. Denial is well established in her personal life.

He is the linguistics expert, with a specialty in semiotics. He excels in interpreting transposed simulacra, while noting conflicting messages. She is an accomplished polyglot, with a specialty in philology. She excels in comparing a diversity of scholarship, while translating in no uncertain terms.

Each has a look which seems perfectly designed to elicit some kind of an inferiority complex in another. It was born in a marketplace, and has become conscious of itself. It is keenly aware of the beauty of youth, extended forever through numerous manipulations.

She will not admit that she has feelings for him...not even to herself. Sometimes, however, she makes a mistake when talking with others and refers to him as her "husband." There is an excess of moisture due to poor circulation...where a fungus is breeding in a room that is humid. A dehumidifier was purchased, but it just keeps running. There is seepage on the walls of a closed-up cellar.

"It began many ages ago. Jove was incensed at Prometheus, who had—with the help of friends—bestowed the civilizing influence of fire upon humanity. He was angered by the Titan's gall, and proceeded to punish him. He was given a continually rejuvenating gall. He decided to make an example of him. He was chained to the summit of Mount Caucasus...where an eagle would visit him daily, and feast upon it. How lovely!

"Earth, however, had sympathy for Prometheus. She sought to comfort him. No one really knows why... She shared with him her knowledge of the possible end of Jove's rule. Of course, it is hard to keep a secret in this pantheon, Dear. Jove became obsessed with acquiring this knowledge. He promised Prometheus many things... He promised him Ganymede. He promised him freedom...if he would divulge what he knew.

"Prometheus did not submit to Jove's surly demand for thousands of years. It is said that he wanted to maintain his dignity against overwhelming odds. He even became a living legend for this act of defiance... 'The Benefactor of Humanity.' He was quite the glamorous rebel. Then, after all of those years, he talked!

"Well, I have the scoop, Dears. It was nothing but a trope, a red herring! Of course, I knew it all along... The story that he confessed was some hackneyed tale of a son that was to be born from a coupling with a mysterious goddess...a son who would be greater than his father, and threaten his rule. It was so perfectly paranoid that he believed it immediately!

Divinity's knowledge of these events, however, was subject to the censorship of Jove. The only existing accounts were offered by a human playwright, written ages later from inspirations received by imbibing at the Pierian Springs. It was these emanations that formed the body of a trilogy called The Prometheia...whose few extant copies were quickly destroyed by the followers of Jove, in case the rest of us might one day discover them.

There was one book that was spared: the first. This decision was not conferred by its obvious erudition, but because it reinforced the consequences of not heeding the authority of his words. Most of the second book has perished, with the exception of several tattered fragments. To be sure, many extrapolations have resulted from the discovery of these literary pieces... Finally, all of the third and final book has been lost, with the exception of this mysterious quote: "quiet, where need is...and talking to the point."

Of course, it is well-known that Prometheus was eventually freed. Still, his closest friends confided that he still felt the shackles of bondage. It is my duty to reveal to you now that he spoke about his feelings on the record, and exclusively to me. He was a wreck, Dears. He was a wreck. It seems that Earth had told him many things, but she hadn't told him all. She spoke in a riddle that provided no answers. She was waxing melancholic...about a message that she had decoded from a signal in her midst, of which she had been previously oblivious. The only revelation that she divulged was a sequence of a process: from the personal to the greater to the universal. It is the nature of augury: It is a dynamic process, fueled by realizing potential. Don't we know that inherent capacity is a potential burden?

"In any case, he didn't know what to do. He was possessed of great foresight, but was in no position to see. There were too many unforseens...too many unknowns. He asked my opinion. I told him that he needed a factual base. He searched the engines; then he searched the stars. He poured himself over diverse books of reference in a faraway place where he could reflect. He wandered into an encyclopaedic daze, into the sight of another. He awoke to the sight of an oracle."

****

Mercury stands upon a well-formed boulder which he prefers to think of as a promontory. He is pleased that nature has sculpted it into masculine, yet fluid dimensions. This artful interplay of energies appeals to him. It makes a bold statement, like a heart-warming meal with a good presentation.

Stirring music reminds him of his office. He is proud of his credentials, but there are too many accolades. It is getting embarrassing... Somehow, he keeps getting mentioned in the news! Such public recognition can be quite tiring. Media coups can be absolutely wounding. After all, he is the official scribe of this pantheon, though his greatest love is for the theater. He is also an expert on period costumes.

Clio is sitting next to him with a quill in her hand. Vengeance is hers! Her hair is pulled-back tightly, and her posture is immaculate. She has begun to hum and efficiently wind a tune around its notes. She is fond of martial songs.

"Welcome to Avernus, the amphitheatre at the base of a precipice. You see...they simply must have a precipice. They refuse to subscribe to any belief that does not include one. Here we gather at the end of the fourth stage of humanity. Some of us are poised. Some of us are not. Some of us may never be, Dear!"

• • •

Dear, I suppose that our throngs of erudite worshippers were just suffering a massive group delusion...

• • •

CHAPTER TWO

A golden box is opened as a voice of wisdom is heard across Earth, reciting a poem...amidst a background of that most bitter kind of dissent...that heinous form of treachery and betrayal that is created by a projection of its own denial, and a lack of accountability... that most despicable comradery, where a denial of a truth that is known and verifiable holds company with a defamation of character, and---promulgated with lies---attempts to secure that which one does not deserve, that which is not one's own, or that for which one is not suited.

A court is convened in an outpost of arrogance
At the edge of an empire of twisted resolve
Where suspicion is honored and held without charges
In a cloak of denial of the nature of sovereign

The calm of consensus is its basis for governance
Where a truth is coerced from a purpose corrupted
As privation of spirit removes access to counsel
And intelligence sequestered is the product of torment.

A long-simmering war of the sexes was renewed across Earth, as each sex was attempting to gain power over the other. The established agreements were no longer applicable; their concomitant rules no longer applied. A focal point developed in the conflict: It was only the ownership of life itself...its conception, maturation and termination.

A tenuous understanding had been made in the preceding millennia to keep the peace. The men would retain an advantaged position, but the interests of women would be insured through contract. The men were expected to ensure their material needs.

The men were expected to protect them from harm. The contract was enjoined in a strange rite of passage, renewed and reviewed throughout the cycles of life. The men would still have the ownership of the women, but the women would control the ideal of the man.

****

Clio rearranges her skirt, which opens onto the audience. She tucks it in slightly under each leg, leaving just enough torque for any available intrigue or voyeurism, simultaneously gauging the response of every interested male audience member. Then, she will subject this focus group to a checklist for interesting characteristics. This is the review that establishes the introductory phase of what will be the inevitable date with the unsatisfying byproduct of her denial: interesting corollaries.

She passes to him an overview to read, labeled, "Abridged History of Humanity."

He continues...reading aloud.

Item #1 A Patriarchy had ruled through the last several stages.

Item #2 It executed authority in enveloping hierarchies.

Item #3 The most desired positions were the ones at the top.

Item #4 Competition was established as the mode of operation.

Item #5 Order was enforced to guard against thuggery.

Item #6 Teamwork was valued to accomplish this goal.

Item #7 Behavior was groomed in playground rituals.

Item #8 A pecking order determined the formation of clubs.

Item #9 The clubs were a means to enforce codes of behavior.

Item #10 Only the males were allowed to be members.

Item #11 They liked to buy gifts for young women with pert breasts. (OMIT!)

Item #12 Girls were restricted to ancillary positions.

Item #13 Women were seen as being part of the territory.

Item #14 They had to be obedient like herds or cute like pets.

Item #15 They were cattle in a fence, or a kindle in a basket.

Item #16 These restrictions increased their desirability as commodities in a market.

"True enough, Dear, and thank you for the cliff notes. What was Item #11, again? It seems to have been omitted..."

"Pas de quoi and move along!"

"Of course, of course...here we are, Dear! We have not seen fit to take an ongoing role in human affairs for hundreds of years. Still, here we are. Our names might be a little different here and there, but a flower is still a flower, and our land is full of lilies. We are in their better poetry and music. We are in their better painting and sculpture. We are the inspiration for their better literature—though it is in short supply."

He holds aloft a trendy cocktail.

Clio raises hers too. A lemon wedge falls to the side, however, as she is preoccupied by a delightful reverie: She is on a working vacation. There are neatly pressed banners waving in front of a judiciary building the day after a cold front has passed. An uncluttered sky is made even more aseptic by streamlined birds flying in perfect formation.

"They tried to eradicate us. They tried to extirpate us. They tried to deny how important we are for civilization. They even tried to remove any semblance of reality from us by saying that we were nothing but myth. Then, they wrote us off in a revised version of classical studies. Dear, I suppose that our throngs of erudite worshippers were just suffering a massive group delusion..."

He flings his hands into the air, flapping them around in mocked unimportance.

"Vulgarities! Vulgarities!"

Clio raises her glass a little too recklessly, spilling some of its contents onto the historical record. She lifts her weight from one foot to the next...in the recurring percussive interlude between the major events of her life: It is the sound of busy shoes covering their tracks. She hopes that he has not noticed.

"Vulgarities! Vulgarities!" He cries again as he throws his hands in front of him, moving his fingers as if to offer crumbs to a possibly capable, but lazy horde.

He stops to perfect a dramatic pause: It is time to indulge a deep-seated need. Eyes open widely to mid-wife its execution, as sleeves recede and arms reach skyward. Exquisite bracelets loop from his wrists, then hang in an arc reaching down from his elbows. There is a wincing of his facial muscles as if an unwanted effluvium has just encroached into his personal space. He has mastered gesticulation: He never tires of this role.

Everything has its place. He clutches a strand of wine-colored plume, peeking from behind it with the glance of a tease. What was once an accessory is now a tool for emphasis. He has only skimmed the surface of historical fiction: Now it is time to read some biographies!

Clio's eyes are lost somewhere in the bombast, and somewhere in the reverie. They easily succumb to the gravitational pull of her own impressive hubris...and close for the moment. There is a smell about her too, too sweet. This always happens in times of psychological motivation: It is the flatulence that sneaks out of a yeasty constitution.

"Earth is retching in the face of disrespect. She has been robbed and degraded. She is being held against her will and mocked. She has even been allotted her own day! How gracious of them. Dear, this subjugation of a celestial one by the spiritual equivalent of the parvenu is difficult for us to watch.

"Just look at them out there. We bring them to you in high definition, like looking out of a window. They can be watched anytime and at any place. There are hundreds of channels yet no entertainment. Still, there is a certain cheap fascination about them, like with gaudy little items that one hides from his sophisticated friends when they walk into a room for fear of being associated with them."

Clio unconsciously grabs her necklace, as he makes the acknowledgement with eye contact...and coolly turns away.

"Look at that one. He has decided to participate in a secular political process. He has decided to vote, but he must wait his turn. He is told to go into a meeting room that is lined with religious symbols. He is led into this church sanctuary, where he sits with everyone—beneath a massive cross—festooned with proselytizing messages. Then, he is sent home and encouraged to anticipate the results of a rigged election. It is a freedom parade which has no spectators. It is a hall of democracy that is built by slaves. They bear watching, Dear. They bear watching.

* *

A noise is coming from a first-aid booth. He knows this people. Their voices are familiar. They are asking for assistance, as they are ready to preach to humanity: They would like to be sponsored. They are preparing to embark into the genocide that is in progress across Earth. There are riches to be made in the rebuilding process...and they are ready to clean-up. They have medicine to sell. They have a new sales pitch, too. They will try to educate persons to try to live life as if it were an infectious disease.

The goddess of tragedy, Melpenome, is their most effective spokesperson. She is particularly qualified, with a degree in nursing and a degree in business. She is all over the place in this day and age. She had already set up a portable clinic for the benefit of the public; now, she is disseminating information. She is promoting this campaign by handing out pamphlets...and giving free advice. Her best advice is to pay for regular check-ups.

BE AWARE OF RISK FACTORS. TRY NOT TO BECOME A STATISTIC. YOU JUST MIGHT BE ABLE TO BUY MORE TIME. REVIEW THESE TENENTS FREQUENTLY. STRESS ONE EVERY THREE MONTHS. THINK OF IT LIKE A BOOSTER PROGRAM! YOU COULD ALWAYS SUCCOMB TO A SILENT EPIDEMIC. REMEMBER, YOU MIGHT STILL BE ABLE TO INFECT, EVEN IF YOU DO NOT EXHIBIT ANY SYMPTOMS.

This information has its own rewarding end: the conference. It is a special service for friends and family members of the patient. It is best when held in a private room where the lights are low... This is the time to tell them that a loved one is very ill. It does not look good from the perspective of the pathogen. In fact, the chances are good that she will not make it. At this point, her eyes will become round, stretched by adrenaline...the drug of choice for emergency services.

The insurance company will not cover a lengthy stay; thus it is time to talk about a living will. In addition, there is really no reason to take life-support measures... Besides, the patient woke-up for a brief time to say that none should be taken. This statement was heard by at least one medical professional. It is a scenario that has been seen so many times that it has become a pattern: She is just trying to let go.

"We are professionals. This is what we do. Do not over-extend yourself. What would happen if you got sick? You look like you could use a hug...

All of this coverage is provided by a group that used to be known as "AIDDIVINE." Still, they needed a new name...one with more vision. Months of daily meetings were endured by the administration until they bravely decided upon "DIVINEAID." This name could more clearly represent the services that they offer...and be more easily recognized by the public. It is a strong brand name.

"DIVINEAID" wants to promote a more healing environment, though it will have to make some painful changes. These are challenging times, and they must remain competitive. Most of these changes should occur through attrition, but they cannot make any promises. Of course, there is always the possibility of making a lateral move to another career-field—where one can be retrained and rehired as a new employee—

without the burden of benefits. Then the distribution of raises will be contingent upon the decoding of acronyms.

The first changes were announced through sports-oriented analogy. The more recent changes, however, have been announced through war-oriented analogy. It has finally decided to centralize most of its functions. There are three main branches of its main operation, as numerous diagrams illustrate this new command. It has even announced its executive officers: Eris is in charge of its administrative branch; Starvation is in charge of its in-patient facility; Mors is in charge of its out-patient facility.

They are usually found in each other's company, easy to spot in business suits of beige and navy-blue. They love to make decisions that affect their employees, though they rarely consult those who are directly affected. Thankfully, their offices have been moved to separate buildings, where they do not have to have daily contact with the patients. They claim to value their employees, however, so they have recently decided to make cosmetic changes to their specific areas: They have covered the walls with pictures of forlorn children waving goodbye to loved ones in automobiles, at train stations and at airports.

This remodeling job is actually part of a master-plan to impress the inspectors of accreditation. There they go, an amorphous blob, spinning about in a commissioned dance. They step past one desk and glide onto the next...then backward to the first. It is a bureaucratic two-step. Their numbers swell as they walk about the buildings, picking-up more bureaucrats as they go. They add administrators, doctors and pharmaceutical salespersons. It is a patrol of accretion, a nervous skid of badges.

Eris seeks a strong presentation, though her hair is wild and untended atop a crude, patchwork face. Her eyes open widely and close dramatically as she speaks. Her pupils look as small as hovering pests, while her voice is raspy...an obsessive remnant from a recent past of screaming at others while abusing amphetamines and binging on alcohol. There is a disturbing hum to inward pulsations that inflames her words like branded convictions.

Starvation pines for the essence of his aspirations and pursuits. There is a frothy exudate that hangs from his mouth, as he claims to have been liberal in his very early youth...though it was gradually benumbed through years of penury. He has unveiled a new diet for the terminally ill: They should never be allowed to have a full stomach. They could become fat! He has an unnerving tendency to sing unintelligibly in a high-pitched sound of strained exhilaration. It is difficult to tell if he is laughing or crying.

Mors is seeking photo opportunities in wounded-spaces. There's a slight little motion of a wispy phantom-tail of hair to an infectious rhythm that rattles around in his mind. It's the slow, painful death that an earworm can cause...where the knees of wildebeests are always buckling to the sound of "The Baby Elephant's Song" at a dried-up hole.

A commercial has been made to promote the recent changes. It will debut in the final phase of the romancing of the inspectors of accreditation, in a town-hall forum that is open to the public. Then, it will be distributed to all of humanity. It is a song that was produced with fictitious former patients, a hoarse reproduction in pursuit of pathos. The crowd holds hands and sways as a chorus, while they praise "DIVINEAID," and refer to them as heroes.

It will run in conjunction with the opening of the new, state-of-the-art facility. It is a kind of a theme-park, a gated community of medical professionals...the creative whimsy of cold science. There are ill-suited partners of barren avenues—denuded of trees—but riddled with saplings. Architectural features stick-out unexpectedly, like a nipple on the back or a finger on a nose. They are unusual, but unimaginative...functional but unappealing, a living space constructed of incomprehensible parts.

• • •

Oh Saturn, you're really killing me now!

• • •

CHAPTER THREE

Blessed be the ties that bind...? What a freak show, Dear! There is a special phrase for the noble, shared blood of this divinity: double-cousins. We are all interrelated at this point. At least, we can claim to be downwardly mobile for generations...though it is now the only tangible connection to our historical parallel: a failed, breakaway republic. Welcome to this lost colony of urban legends, whose eternal gratitude is bestowed upon the loose cannons which comprise its defense. We shall only hope for the release of mass hysteria...

"Pssst! Pssst!"

There's a reporter's relish like a clap of thunder. Cerulean flashes mean concealment and collusion. Brief moments pass in inadvertent stares...in a kind of a face-off, a silent sense of acknowledgement. It is important to achieve journalistic accuracy: Misinformation is spread from authorities; interviews are read like coached performances; inauspiciously, even scientific polling has a three-percent rate of error. Still, some things are timeless in a field that is crowded, soothing the mind like a reassertion of recidivism in the lack of randomness of an unsolicited demographic survey: Do not believe it unless you have heard it yourself.

"One was born high. One was born low. Of course, Miss Pandora was born low, low, low. She has so much eternity now and knows not what to do with it. Just look at those flowers in her hat! I am surprised that she doesn't have the whole mess tied-up behind her head in a garish bow. Simple daisies crave reflective wrapping; bows secure the uninspired sentiment.

"It is said that her hat is the lure of many a brawny woodsman."

His mind immediately transports him to a distant time, as his tongue unconsciously slides to the bottom of his teeth. He imagines a stump-riddled foot-path beside flowing water, with a background of coral-colored, chalky rock. There is an exotic forest-dweller standing close to the water's edge, in a quaint clearing of what looks like Japanese Painted Ferns. The steady sounds of manly contests and ritual chanting set the context, emboldened by a full, sweeping orchestral introduction. His penis is wrapped in a tropical plant frond, while feathers in his hair reinforce his gamesmanship.

The orchestra slowly fades to a thumping syncopation, thrilling him with the effect of the visceral...more immediate than with theater. He tilts his head as he has heard a rustling off the trail. He offers a well-timed shriek—with a shaking of the branches—and the race is on! He is betrayed by his coxcomb, a bright, red beacon filtered through the brush. He is being pursued by the scourge of the primitive. Oh! The tip of the arrow can be so smart! We, too, have lived in Acadia! We, too, have lived in Acadia!

Pandora grabs Minerva by the hand. She has just received a tip that the new commercial is about to air. Minerva will have a higher impression of her once she sees this work. After all, she was honored by a request from the producers to be the liaison to humanity. They said that she had an instinct for it: She was the one who could capture humanity's essence. Her instinct was to request pallets full of tight-fitting clothing of manmade fibers, while warmth would be provided by rabbit-fur coats. They even agreed to grant her one humble request: the title of Esthetician. It was thrilling and confusing at the same time, like running-up and asking another to hold her place in line at a crowded retail store.

It can hardly be heard past the roar of humanity. Their numbers are staggering. She forgets her coaching, like a slap on the back from behind, or a dog's cold nose at the crotch. She's tired of it. She's gonna tell it...and she don't care who hears it. She's gonna rip 'em a new one! She's gonna scratch that thing that's been itchin'. She's gonna burn a hole in their favorite chair, and she's gonna wiggle her index finger around in the air as she does. She's gonna chew on her gums a little bit too.

She turns toward humanity, and puts a hand on her hip. Then, she takes her free hand, and blows them a kiss. The air around her is heavy—like a sandwich spread—as she reaches up to grasp it...as preserving a keepsake. Instead, she captures it! She digs into it... and brings it down slowly to her outstretched rear end. She smacks it good and she smacks it hard.

"We should be your heroes!

"Do you hear me?"

So many thoughts race through Minerva's head. Somehow, she still feels shocked... It isn't the way that it was supposed to be. She had led the cause to support humanity... She had the full support of well-meaning brethren. She conspired with Prometheus to give them the sparks; now, she felt somewhat responsible for their lack of adjustment. Two things were clear: They gave them these gifts which they could not receive, as they took from them ignorance, humanity's privilege.

They never adjusted to the new situation. Ontogeny continued to recapitulate phylogeny. They even misunderstood why they weren't getting better. The universe seemed to reward ugly behavior, step-by-step, in stages of development. The cycles of violence ratcheted upward alongside history's mistakes, like earthen pyramids long-abandoned by their creators' descendents, who now grow corn in abandoned plazas for their new conquerors.

A well-meaning mind can be skewed by a bleeding heart. Everything must be worthy of appreciation and interest, even if the facts have to be misrepresented. It is an exercise in futility that can be challenging, like superimposing abstractions upon a literal landscape, removing them from their context...strategies shaped upon feelings, confounded. Then, drop it on the floor and rearrange it, mix and match...deconstruct it: The truth will drop out of a thing turned inside-out.

Examine oneself as if looking in a mirror; discern one's motives by questioning the image. Abstruseness is the path of a harmony of spirit, as infirmity will become strength in a thoughtful society. Ultimately, the crutch will become the tool of enfranchisement and power. Strength will be equated with encroaching decrepitude—or with its association—like choosing to live below a roomful of persons...each of whom is walking with a cane. It is hardly a sacrifice!

There is an exaggerated sense of self-importance, a perfectionism so deeply believed that the discovery of imperfection is seen as failure. There are the frailties of existence, the flaws of character. Still, infinite choices lie in front of them, as possibility is born of choices made. Empathy is perfect in its validation of suspicion: they are powerful beings, but unworthy of the ability. Thus, the question of pain has no satisfactory answer, and the positive ritual is only a shield. An affirmation of these truths reveals the obvious: Assume responsibility for every ill; proclaim a guiltiness for every offense.

• • •

It is like what happens in a Stockholm Syndrome: Victims crave the attention of victimizers. Their culture was no longer a worthy receptacle; thus, they retreated beyond the peeled walls of dereliction…captives whose past was heavy with the burden of oppression. There is a red-hot guilt, expiated through subservience: Their heritage is gauged by their association with humanity's misery.

They became obsessed with images and causes in this quest to show concern. It was decided that they should be more like humanity as a commitment to this solidarity. Eventually, they would have to sacrifice something vital to their identity. The most obvious, associative characteristic to this identity was their voice…this crucible of refinement.

They had assimilated thousands of words from the various languages under their purview, creating the greatest lexicon that is known to exist…affording them with a word for almost every nuance of experience. Concomitantly, they discovered and ascertained the patterns of mellifluousness in which these nuanced notions could be more beautifully expressed.

The pain associated with hearing it was now excruciating, however. The sacrifice was begun immediately, as this prism-like discourse was cheerfully dismantled in favor of the simplicity of pidgin-variants. It was particularly exhilarating to see how quickly something that took so long to build can fall. Finally, they could retreat to the background and never be seen, covert narrators gone into hiding.

"It is like that recurring dream. I am led into a grand hall, crowded with dignitaries. My date walks me out to the finest table in the dining area. I have a nagging feeling that something is out of place… I get up from the table to visit the powder room, but everyone is watching me as I walk away. I look down to discover that I am wearing only under-clothing.

"You should surely consult an expert, Dear. Many of your dreams are quite strange. Worse, they are not uncommon. Morpheus is one of my closest friends... He just might be able to help you, though I shall not make any promises. Perhaps you might stop eating too close to bedtime. The clothes that you wear may be getting too tight. A body will beg you to let it breathe!

* *

Something about Prometheus had begun to plague him... He talked of his desires, but he talked about the females. He would look at him, but he would talk about them. He thought that Pandora looked good, too. She was just what he liked... He liked them when they needed some work. He called them a "handyman's special": The more work the better.

He didn't believe Prometheus. Besides, it seemed to him that he would talk about her when he was angry with him. Of course, he was just trying to see if he could make him jealous... He was only interested in Pandora as a gauge, as the way that he could satisfy his need to know that he, Saturn, had feelings for him. It made perfect sense... Just connect the dots.

Besides, his intuition could not be wrong; the bond was too strong. They were meant to be together. Each of them was like a pulp that possessed an eager longing to be eviscerated from the fruit of the other's passion. He even thought that this fruit would be reddish-purple, like the giant plums that grow in California, and south of its border.

He continued his pursuit... He wanted to honor Prometheus. He was still thinking about what he had said about the females. Somehow, it was related to the augury...something to do with the cycle of energy: He remembered being told that he was only using half of the tools that were required to complete it. It bothered him. It made him feel insecure. It reminded him of painted whirly-gigs sprouting from a newly cleared field. He could almost picture them as they were spinning in the wind.

It reminded him of the stories that he had heard from the other males. They talked of a "wild and imperative allurement" of a preponderance of feminine energy. They were so full of desire when they talked that they became very beautiful, very swarthy. Still, he had not really tried or wanted to take things to that level... Perhaps he had just not proceeded far enough into the sequence of events. Perhaps it could be natural, like being in heat.

Then he had a notion: He didn't want to put conditions on love. He wanted to be true to himself...and he didn't want to deny. Besides, denial inhibited augury. He would study these rituals and pursue that pathos. He would search the fine lines of fluidity and saturation through any peephole that was necessary.

He might make different associations. Mix it all up. What if he approached a female from the side that held something in common with the males? What if he thought of this "backside" as he thought that the majority of males would be thinking in this situation? What if he pictured these beautiful males in his mind as he thought about how excited they were? They would look rough behind the edges. They would need a little work.

What if he thought of them—objectified them—into things that needed to be filled? What if these objectified repositories needed to be filled with joy and excitement? What if he viewed these rituals, and turned-up the sound...with a close-up of unassociated hungry mortars and a variety of erect and distended pestles in a montage? Theoretically, he could train himself to respond in a Pavlovian way to the sounds of friction between all appendages and apertures. They could be tingling, squealing, super-holes. Was this the way most of the males felt when considering this type of union? Is this the sequence of thought—or steps—that went through their minds?

Perhaps he could think of them like the callas. They could be a beautiful hybrid, an energizing orange with a retaining angle, a receptacle for dew. It could be like a warm patch of moist ground, welcoming visitors. The stalk could be the body. The flower could be the organ. Of course, they could be seen as flowers on a stalk, sitting in a garden, greeting their visitors with hospitable colors...intermediaries between the virile males and him.

The possibilities were thrilling. Could he experience this energy in a vicarious manner? Then, could he experience it on his own? He suspected that these might not be the processes by which a male generally approached a female. Still, he could feel the rush of the theoretical allurement... Perhaps he could hear the sirens' sweet song.

He confided in Minerva, and told her of his work. He remembers that she laughed. It was uncharacteristic of her to mock an honest pursuit. She even thanked him. He remembers her laughing and laughing and finally saying "Oh, Saturn, you're killing me."

He continued with his discourse. In theory, one could, at this point, represent an excess of masculine energy. This energy would have to have—almost uncontrollably—an excess of feminine energy to feel whole. It would just happen automatically... At this point, Minerva could not help herself.

"Oh Saturn, you're really killing me now!"

Admittedly it did seem rather odd. Besides, he just didn't feel the desire. Somehow, his theoretical allurement seemed to be contingent upon his interpretation of—and the subsequent attachment to—the desires of the beautiful males. He didn't want it to be like the hoar-frost chill of that high, come-hither voice, or the sight of that quivering, too soft skin.

He remembers Clio's advances; he couldn't possibly forget. She would accompany Mercury when he would visit him clandestinely. She began to offer to help him with his research... She said that she was in a unique position to help him, as she had maintained an impressive portfolio of statistics from her own research...one that he could peruse.

He was fascinated by this opportunity to compare his findings with those from a different perspective. Of course, everyone approaches a subject with his or her own proclivities...and it was obvious that she was a dedicated collator: He had not considered using facial scars and abdominal tattoos as vital prerequisites for the subjects of his studies.

Still, he began to feel uncomfortable... She insisted that he accompany her in drink, saying that it would take the edge off of the numbers. Gradually, she became more irritable...wanting to talk less about the actual research, and more about its attendant anecdotes. Her words began to slur as she told a joke that had something to do with a blue-bird, a red-bird and a swallow. There was even a barely comprehensible discourse about the similarities between making love to a woman and eating spaghetti. Then an old and embellished photograph of her—almost nude—and taken from behind...while wearing nothing but a silk scarf, dropped -out from between the two most important papers in her portfolio, labeled "conclusion."

Finally, he almost collapsed from a downdraft of fermented breath as ten drunken little fingers tried to undo his zipper. He tried to stand—to run away—but she leaped onto his lap, lifting her wrinkle-free skirt to expose a bald patch of ground... It unfurled right in front of him, like a floppy red-flag that had been left out too long in the rain...flapping in the wind for an unrequited allegiance.

He quickly shook her off his leg, as she rolled-over on the floor...straightened her clothes, and walked away as if it had never happened.

• • •

It was a ghost-ship, commandeered by one of her incarnations, spreading her message while traveling the sea by downdrafts of pity.

• • •

CHAPTER FOUR

Thus began this 'Age of Information,' in a reassertion of feminine energies, carried in on the padded shoulders of non-impartial witnesses. A watershed was reached in an obsession for the details of a famous woman's life. She was revered like a goddess with a royal flush of parced-out alleles, from an unlikely kingdom of recessive genes. She had classical poise, intelligence and beauty. It was said that she lived a storybook life.

Pandora and Eris grew jealous of her fame. How dare she be treated like a goddess on Earth, while they were not supposed to influence events? They said that what is now considered nobility was still divinity's trash. They created misunderstanding in her personal life, and made her problems fodder for public fascination. Finally, they declared emotion to be the language of the soul, while they declared the imperative to be "emotionally honest."

She was homegrown, suckled at the entertainment outlets, the teats of the media. She was nourished by their attention, and validated by their approval. She arose in an unlikely scenario, from humble beginnings to enormous wealth. It was an almost perfect situation: The highs and lows of her life could be measured from childhood until death.

Then, she quit playing by the rules. Humanity loves a winner, but a winner must work hard to stay on top. She began to seek her own personal relationships, potential filler from absent agendas. She was still beloved, but she had gone too far...blinded in her apostasy: She sought her primary satisfaction in these relationships. She had begun to ignore her most important covenant with the ones who had made her famous: Her most important covenant should always be with her consumers.

There was agreement in the public discourse that something was terribly wrong with her. Now, she would have to seek help. It was only in her best interest to be stopped in her quest for the destruction of her own image. There should be an intervention of ridicule...a vilification of her as ugly... Astonishingly, eyewitnesses were reporting that she was on the verge of being fat!

The news arrived amidst a litany of child abductions, alleged rapes and celebrity addictions. An automobile has been tracked and pursued...and verified to be transporting the new goddess as she tries to explore her new life. They are only trying to see how far she has fallen... They frighten her as they pursue her, shouting to her for answers to their questions. Suddenly, her automobile is surrounded...crushed, filmed and catalogued. They continue to ask her questions even though she is unresponsive. Finally, a prefabricated video tribute to her life is played.

They knew what ugliness their jealousy had caused. Still, they could not acknowledge it. They would not admit it: It was personal to them. Instead, they paid enormous homage to her existence. They eulogized her by burning a candle in the wind, in denial of the collective breath that had extinguished it. Then, they hid the evidence under sympathy notes and flowers in the street.

It started propitiously as a fight for equality. They wanted the right to control their own bodies. It was supposed to stop the bloodletting of the masculine energies. It was supposed to nurture. It was supposed to heal. It was supposed to restore the lost balance of power: It was supposed to stop the violence.

Ironically, the struggle was seen in a universal context, but could only be understood when discussed in "female spaces." They wrote books on the subject, and formed clubs to discuss it. They shouted "misogyny!" but never heard of "misandry." A strict code of behavior would now be required for the grooming of the young women: These theories should be mandated in classrooms and schools, whose syllabuses will be prerequisites for the ultimate goal: a rewriting of history.

It will be highly addictive like chocolate and melodrama. The emotional bond is of primary importance, while the personal relationship is the most important unit. Of course, it will require the establishment of an ideal of a perfect, selfless love: the mother-child bond. They had already chosen names for their brave, future daughters.

Soon, an anomaly had developed in the study of the doctrine. Sex was not expression, but an extension of politics... Still the behavior of males continued to be a problem: Their expression was not bound by emotional needs. They had desires that were clear and unfettered, like those of the un-cuddly animals. They were dirty, like pigs. They were wanton, like dogs. Things would be so much better if they acted like voles. There were other warning signs, too: Lying on top always equaled dominance; the act of penetration was equivalent to rape.

They really just wanted to avoid a commitment. After all, a committed relationship is the consummate achievement...the most important thing that one can do with one's life. A name can only be verified by an "and" on either side of it; then, a person's "true" identity can be known. It is part of the captivating rewrite: this great, heroic epic, where the pursuit of the "life partner" is like the slaying of a dragon.

Intuition will be the heroine's guide. She will know it immediately because it will register in her heart: She will have her other half! The only requirement is to follow a path that is written in the stars, this milky confluence whose treacherous waters must be navigated for this sole purpose of existence. Then, it will not be a meeting; it will be a reunion.

The holiest day of the year will be declared to be Valentine's Day. Moreover, the most grievous penalty in the new history will be for infidelity. In fact, it will be a crime. Of course, infidelity can be both physical and emotional. Each man who has committed an infidelity to a woman will be forced to stand up and renounce his infidelity. He will be forced to state how much he respects his wife or girlfriend, even if she has perpetrated violence against him.

Next, his confession shall culminate in a plea for forgiveness, not only from his wife or girlfriend, but from every woman in the world. Then, his delivery and style will be dissected to examine whether he seems to show sufficient sincerity. Furthermore, his body language will be studied to ascertain if he displays any features of resentment, or dishonesty. Finally, it will be necessitous to note if this confession has been over-practiced.

Finally, his penalty can be mitigated if he chooses to submit to one of two options, or both options...at the same time, or in close succession. Firstly, he will have to admit that his sexual crime was perpetrated by an addiction to sexual experiences, and the creative freedom which fosters it. Then, he can either voluntarily agree to submit to sexual rehabilitation, or he can wait until it is his sentence. Secondly, he will begin what will probably be a lifelong drug-therapy – administered by a sex-addiction therapist – which will dramatically curb these desires. Thankfully, a faithful adherence to treatment will likely produce perfect compliance with the rules of monogamy.

Of course, the strongest relationships will still have problems. Conflict-resolution is a popular subject in this burgeoning new science. Hyphenated phrases suggest cozy solutions, an inner-connectedness oblivious to autonomy. Females are better than males at this, too. Remember, disagreements are solved by finding common ground: It is easy to agree when you blame someone else.

It had been like this since the beginning. There was an imprint on a template, an x-linked gene passed through the father's line. Night felt close to her sister, Earth. Still, she was unnerved by the accomplishments of her offspring. She couldn't stand the thought of good associations being made with those other than her own. They were her flesh and blood. They were her flesh and blood! The more ancient times saw her grow leery of Eurynome's children. Eurynome was the lover of the ruler, Ophion. Then, after Ophion was dethroned by Saturn, she grew leery of Rhea's children too.

She caused all kinds of problems. She didn't want anyone else's offspring to excel, yet she tried to keep her own out of sight. It just wasn't as she had planned it. Some of hers were always different... They had a morbid sensibility, a fascination with limits. She was afraid of what they might expose in the blank slate of untouched palette. She tried to hide them under her cloak. She would draw a curtain when they left the lights on... They didn't mix well in polite company; they seemed to be missing the faculty for discretion: They would say anything to anyone at anytime.

They were hurt by their mother's lack of acceptance, and they felt an imperative to talk about their problems. They organized their siblings to have an intervention... Of course, they loved a crowd and craved attention. Soon, they broadened the concept, and invited the world. They pioneered the tell-all format of the talk-show forum. There, they found a massive audience of displaced emotion. Eventually, they perfected the art of public humiliation.

"Honey, did he, your own kin, force himself on you?"

A short pause ensues.

"Yes! Yes, he did!"

"Honey, did he, your own kin, hurt you?"

A short pause ensues.

"Yes! Yes, he did!"

"Honey, I know that this might be difficult for you, but we need to know something else... We need to know everything so that we can help you, honey."

A short pause ensues.

"Okay, I'm sorry. Okay. I'll try..."

"Honey, did he—the one who hurt you—have a large penis?"

* *

He had to say something: He wanted to know. He wanted to honor his feelings. He tried to unlock the unspoken... He told Prometheus that he enjoyed his attention. Now, he wanted his affection... He had a compulsion to tell him.

He asked him to follow him into the ocean stream, to an island across the water. There, a mountain of rock arose from this bath. He knew it well...and loved to ascend it. He would listen to a music with a rhythm that seemed steady, but gradually revealed an increasing tension. There was the sound of a cello, always soothing. It went to a place in the unconscious mind to those emotions that are seldom acknowledged, but reaffirming and vital. It reminded him of fulfilling a long-term goal. He wanted to fulfill it with Prometheus.

They embarked to trade winds that seemed made to melt impasses. He imagined members of their families blessing their journey. They passed beyond the Atlas Mountains, and sailed above the ocean stream. There was no reason to follow instructions: They would ride a massaging current, a sweet effleurage to accomplished art in concordant settings.

His face turned red with the hope of experience... Then, he suggested that they light at its base for a joyous hike. They climbed and he talked. The more that he talked, the more necessary it became... The feeling that he had for him was different than that for anyone else! This was the way that he had wanted to feel! He had recognized him from the moment that they met! He fell in love with him at that instant!

Something felt wrong. He had been here before. Prometheus said nothing. There were channels of silence, parallel lines with no vanishing point, parallel forever in a visual field. He could feel his reservations as he continued to talk, but Prometheus wouldn't listen... It seemed as if he couldn't even hear him. Still, he tried to force the subject. He became too accommodating. He tried to induce that special feeling...all the way to the top of that mountain.

He had thrown caution to the winds, but the winds had changed. They were dry and strong and unseasonably cold. They picked-up sand and began to chafe, stinging his naked legs from behind. His lips felt cracked and his chest unprotected: He had a very male itch.

Prometheus was silent. He seemed obsessed with the possibility that someone might notice them...scanning the horizon for anomalous features, keeping track of the shadows of bushes and trees. There was no acceptance of his feelings. There was no affirmation of his heart. There was no validation of their bond.

The sky turned dark and ugly, like particle board over polished wood. Prometheus turned back... It was time for them to leave, though they had just arrived. He followed Prometheus from a disappointing distance, several steps behind. He retraced this route that had seemed so hopeful, back down a path...a destructive march to the sea, an anaconda system.

He was looking for definition, but got something different. It nudged, but couldn't occupy. It was indefinable space, like worrying in a dream about the experiences in a previous dream. It was some kind of reenactment. Still, he wanted Prometheus to know how he felt...how much he had hurt him. He began to fantasize about a response: It could be highly effective, passive-aggressive, a little ravaged ruin sent in a letter—put aside upon reading—an emotion bomb packed with sharp little nails for cumulative damage.

He looked into the offing as Prometheus took flight...too tired to move, too anxious to sleep. He just lay in the sand and listened to the sounds... It seemed as if a voice were coming from the sea. He was still somewhat lucid to interpret the words...travelling with ease from the crests of the waves, liminal transcripts that presage a dream.

Clinging in constraints of time
Just beyond a fertile shore
Stung by blistered grains of sand
On windward sides in acid soils
A voice is heard upon the wind
From sunken eyes in sallow squalls
Through landscapes fraught with empty hulls
To submersibles that could not rise
With crews upon an unlit floor
Melpenome will climb aboard
To disembark this journeyed crew
By lines of precious coins lost
With maps that lead these uninformed
To scratch a soft spot still disturbed
And seek a place to place a blame
Then build a house with hurt inside
Of things unsaid and left undone
And never let the issue rest
And stir the pot to help sustain

There, put upon a weathered shelf

And stored in quarrels unresolved

A labeled life with caveats

"Warning! Never mix with sweet repose!"

Such life that feeds upon itself

Extracts a pulp from hope removed

Like blood from turnips, grown in salt

Preserved in thoughts of life's regrets

This harvest with a bitter taste

A perfect food for troubled times

So sweet to taste in times of angst:

Adrenaline, the self-consuming fruit.

There was a form that looked like a vision, in a strangely driven trawler—drawing closer and closer—lowering nets into the water. These were not the kinds which seek individual specimens. These could drag the bottom, taking everything and everyone. It was a ghost-ship, commandeered by one of her incarnations, spreading her message while traveling the sea by downdrafts of pity, corrupting the realms of Neptune from an exercise in navigating fluidity and uncertainty to enhance empathy and voice, into spreading a fear of the unknown of a perpetual storm with an intent to deceive.

It is a vehicle of a ruinous methodology... She has so much potential...grace, intelligence and beauty: the whole package. She can go anyplace with anyone; in essence, she will light-up a room. She will entrance her guests with a sovereignty of diction, and an ease of culture. She will charm them with the personal details and timelines of her dearest, most meaningful dreams...until they want her to be happy, until they want her to succeed. Then, her mood will begin to change... She will display an increased sense of agitation, and an enveloping unhappiness...the feelings of helplessness upon that which is unrealized. Gradually, this repetition of vocalized imagery of the unfulfilled will lull them into a trance of melancholy, until they are awakened by an explosion of her histrionics. Ultimately, they will do everything that they can to help her, though it is not her intent to help herself, or to accept theirs.

She wants to hurt. She wants to fail. She wants to feel the pain of hurt, and she wants others to feel her pain. Finally, their sympathetic ears will be seized as evidence for their presumed participation in her misfortune: They have never done anything to help her; at least, they could have always done more.

She has gotten out there early. She is closer to shore than she would normally be, and she has found a fresh harvest: The waters are full of emotional hostages and prisoners-of-love. They are looking for life-boats, but have locked them away—tangled-up tightly—bound to conditions with proffered refrains of solicitous co-dependency.

"Look what you have done to me...

"You make me physically ill!

"You have blood on your hands!"

He didn't want to go there... He just wanted to know. He could feel an encroachment of a creeping dullness that played in the background of a wakeful daze, but ratcheted upward as he would try to recline. It had seemed that their energies were made for each other... Prometheus was more active in the beginning, and more passive in the end. He, himself, was more passive in the beginning, and more active in the end. It played over and over in his mind.

• • •

In fact, it does matter who one likes and dislikes! It is a truth that is found through emotional consensus.

• • •

CHAPTER FIVE

The fate named Atropos is beginning to stir...acting as if something is beginning to move. A thread of energy is clinging to her hand, limning along a ripple of augury. She raises her shears to reach for the thread... Still, nothing...some of life is only a dress rehearsal, Dear... always remember to keep the dress!

"And the shoes...

"We shall not forget about the shoes, Dear...

"A prominent theatre critic has even arrived: His is the seat of all kinds of perfidy! There is a smell of urgency in the unhealthful air...one last check with a meeting in the green room. The scenery is ready; the props are in place. Humanity is on view, but its setting has been optimistically altered: It is framed by a Corinthian colonnade that sprays outward from a proscenium arch.

"Terpsichore leaps about with interpretive dance for the culturally impaired, as the smell of patchouli hovers about her. Goddesses of Love in long hair support her with a subtext of gestures of goodwill and charity to humanity...in case a mass cleansing is necessary. One is carrying a basket of cones—dipped in herbal oils—which shall be set afire and inserted into their ears: It is supposed to awaken a sixth sense in these creatures that cannot filter properly through five. Another is stacking rose-colored quartz and sage into the base of an altar of a heart-shaped bowl, which has just been consecrated with her menstrual blood. It is hoped that their negative thoughts can be guided into this altar, and then released...

"Slowly, figures are made more prominent by the urgency of an orange glow, cast from behind. Bright lights above illuminate these silhouettes as a well-muscled demi-god tenderly removes his cape. These lights are show lights! An unusually small genius runs out to bang a Levantine gong.

"One moment...headdress, please!

"Thank you, Dears! How do you like it? It was secured for me in a mystical land beyond the isles of the blessed by a former lover who still yearned for my touch. It seems that he wanted to prove his love to me by forsaking his current lover, who was soon to become a Sapa Inca, and for whom it was to crown his coronation. I have saved it for centuries, just to wear for you today. It is called a llautu, and the unusual feathers that form its crest were procured from a most reclusive bird, the coraquenque, which lived in the distant lands of this empire, where they were hermetically sealed...then brought to the royal palace, fixed upright...and set in gold.

"It was said that this king of the sun would wear his outfits exactly one night, after which, they would be immediately burned. Dear, what a prima donna! It was at this event that the object of my spurned affection conspired to fete his lover-king to a mad, all night orgy involving the most delectable members of the royal guards, and with whom they enjoyed themselves immensely by imbibing copious amounts of the derivatives of coca leaves, and ayahuasca from a ram's horn.

"Then, just as he fell asleep from exhaustion in his partner's arms, he dreamed of a great fire that was burning amidst a reflection of a house that was floating upon reeds in the water, whose vision was so stunning that it startled him and awakened him. He looked beside their bed—where the headdress had been placed—and it was gone. Instantaneously, he rushed out of their chamber to smell the flames of the sacred pyre outside, to which he fled so daringly that the final steps had to be made close to the ground, with a scarf covering his mouth...to avoid the suffocating smoke. There, he proceeded to snatch it from the hands of the most loyal courtesan of the new emperor – over the terrible screams of 200 sacrificial virgins – and from the perilous heat, just before it hit the flames. Next, he hid his theft in a vicuna hide, and rushed to the owner of a waiting llama caravan to whom he paid an outrageous price to transport it over the most barren terrain...where he had arranged for virile, black-eyed messengers to relay it swiftly on foot, hand-to-hand, over unsound boulders and the terraced gardens of hills, until the hills turned to mountains...which were traversed only via suspension bridges which hung perilously between their peaks above the passes...and all of the way to the shores of Lake Titicaca, where it was hoisted atop a massive golden disk in effigy of our love, as the high altitude and ice crystals combined to form a Turneresque sunrise.

"Of course, Dear, I never saw him again...but I did send one of my emissaries to his self-imposed shrine, to accept his gift. Isn't it the gayest thing that you've ever seen?"

"In any event, welcome to the end of an era!

The little genius runs out onto the stage to hand the emcee a hastily written note:

"It is an official attendance estimate; practically every god, goddess, demi-god and demi-goddess!"

Clio raises her drink.

"Thank you, Dear. Be careful not to spill any...

"We are proud to announce an enormously popular choral ensemble, who are unequalled in the traditional classical repertoire. They have performed in every palace of grandeur. They have garnered the highest prizes in the most renowned competitions. They are no strangers to reviews which include descriptions such as triumphant, rhapsodic and evocative."

"Today, they will perform the world premiere of a work that was commissioned specifically for this event. I have been told that it is a light classic in the tradition of the sailing cultures of the hyperborean regions: It is meant to highlight the love of polyphonic forms that are found in these parts.

"Remember, all of our activities are now funded from private sources. In order to ensure that we are able to continue to bring you entertainment of the highest caliber—and that you are able to receive it—donations are always welcomed. Now, let us greet 'Les Muses.'"

"A dark-eyed demigod

"On Barbary Coast

"Loves caudian forks

"From his Scythian hosts:

"Hot-buttered supper-roll

"Tyrrhenian plum

"Home-grown honey-dew

"Tight-as-a-drum."

This boisterous piece is performed as a round. Each sister sings her melody while only occasionally stopping or starting at the same time. Clio, however, sings her part with a personal interest as she stomps her feet and claps her hands. Her mind seems focused upon salty tales and sailing men; her nostrils are spread outward in a sweet straining, as a nautical mile.

Unfortunately, he is staring at her. She stops for a moment and rechecks her hair; then, she resumes...but only taps the ground lightly until they have finished. She must walk past him to resume her reporting, though the tips of her shoes are warm and hard-pressed.

He makes a mental note about her performance. She certainly brought to it an instinctive brio. Somehow, however, it was a little too much. The skin between her body angles shook like that on a person who eats too much pork. It was like saying "goodnight," with a quick embrace, only to be pulled closer by an unwanted, hip-grinding hug...or a friend who wants to talk with you when she is drunk, slurring her words while saying hurtful and nasty things...just before bedtime, for maximum impact. Then, the next time that she sees you, she will act as if nothing has happened. She will still call you her best friend.

He just had to say it...

"How did that little number go again, Dear?

"Hot-buttered supper-roll

"Tyrrhenian plum

"La-la-la-la-la

"...Tight-as-a-drum?"

Things are still a little strained between these two. They had arranged an exclusive interview with Saturn, which would encompass a series of talks for a delayed release date...sometime during the ratings period. This would be big! It might even reestablish the sovereignty of the ubiquitous grapevine in this time of challenges from independent upstarts. He would conduct the interview, and she would provide factual support.

The topic was Saturn's research for his study of the cycles of energy. He had begun the process of distilling the most meaningful trends and proclivities from the volumes of his fieldwork documents, stacked like a sticky filo pastry full of spicy details. He was particularly interested in male sexual organs... He was fascinated by the variety that he had found in the field: It was part of his life's work.

He noted that the subjects whose ancestry originated in the northern regions had organs that would grow nicely when distended. Curiously, however, they had a tendency to shrink into the body when exposed to cold temperatures or frightening circumstances. It was a plump, fertile grain seeking shelter in its chaff. It was like a winter wheat, tinted softly pink or rose.

He discussed this attribute with Minerva. He told her of his theory that it was some kind of an adaptive trait, or a protective mechanism. He noted that the rivers of this region were cold, while the air temperatures could get frigid. Thus, exposed skin was susceptible to frostbite. She reiterated that she had never been interested in male sexual organs. Still, she noted that it was an interesting theory...like that of the steatopygia that she had found in women of child-bearing years in her own distant travels.

Still, he wondered about the surprise that he had uncovered later in the deeper, equatorial regions...The organs on these subjects were also quite nice. In fact, they were generally larger and longer than those of the other subjects. They bore darker flourishes, embodying the changes of hue in the mixture of red and blue wavelengths, with an emphasis on indigo and magenta.

It was in these lands where he perfected the classic method of research. He used it in the stairwells that led in from the streets. First, the young men would climb them, "I tell you..." Next, their fathers would climb them too, a little out-of-breath, "I tell you..." Finally, their fathers' fathers would wait at the base...and prod him with a drink, "It will feel good!" Experience had taught them to go to completion.

The biggest surprise lay ahead, however. Some of the big ones hardly seemed to grow upon becoming distended. They hardly seemed to grow at all. Some of the biggest ones just changed consistency. Then, he discovered something almost unbelievable: Some of the biggest ones even shrank a little. They actually shrank! He was filled with question... What would be the adaptive trait of this mechanism?

"I don't call that a surprise. I call that a disappointment, Dear.

He did not disagree with this assessment. Still, he had found that if one were to get too emotionally involved in predicting outcomes of research, the results of one's study might become skewed. He would rather follow a scientific method. Give yourself freely to that which you seek... Pay attention to what is statistically important. Let the data determine the research.

Clio was ready to talk. She hadn't enjoyed an interview like this one in a long time; it made her feel like herself again. She wanted to talk about male organs, too. She wanted to talk about how close she had gotten to Prometheus'. She, too, had labored on sacred ground. Besides, it was so embarrassing that she just had to tell it. They would love it!

He was out. She walked in, and she walked around. Somehow, she felt drawn to a particular room. She sneaked into it, as quiet as a nosy one who creeps just closely enough to a hushed conversation to proclaim offense at what was heard. It was wild but soothing, like nature sounds coming from a night-light. She had found his private chamber, but she wanted more... She was on a surveillance mission: She had to find the source. She found it at the foot of his bed...a piece of clothing that one wears closest to his groin. She reached for it as she sat down. She felt rumpled...but began to recline. She lay back until Prometheus' worn undergarment made contact with her nostrils, twitching like those of a hare that is getting ready to nestle. It was so good—almost perfect—like a panacea.

"Clio! Clio! Is that you? What are you doing?"

She couldn't see. Everything was off-white. She felt out of place, like a buried lead. She jumped to her feet in the muted light. She had a headache—so it seemed morning—but she couldn't tell. She couldn't tell anything. Something was draped over her head, and covered it. Prometheus knew what it was, because he wasn't wearing any...

They didn't want to listen to her story, however. They were such busy connoisseurs...They talked about the ones that were quite dry, with a long finish, puckery as tannin. Then, there were those that would drip like a spoon pulled slowly from the top of a fresh jar of honey. They used words like copious, aroma and bouquet. Someone even mentioned hot, buttered rum. They talked about baskets and they talked about lunch.

It was not long before she showed-up on the talk-show. She was furious... She felt like tiny metal teeth slowly chewing-up a tall metal pole. It was supposed to be a routine appearance, a scheduled event. It was part of the publicity surrounding the interview. She was supposed to call it a "bombshell." Instead, she began to cry... She had a "bombshell" all her own.

"Honey, what's wrong? Have they offended you?"

"Yes, yes."

"Have they offended you in a sexual way?"

"Yes, they did."

"What did they do to you, honey? What did they do to you?"

"They talked about male sexual organs while they completely ignored me."

"You poor thing. Do you know that you will have to live with the consequences of their behavior for the rest of your life?"

The talk-show audience agreed. Offensive behavior was now open to a wide interpretation. They decided that they had been ignored, too. They had been ignored, and they had been offended. They traded stories of their victimization. Someone suggested that Clio seek counseling. They crowded together and held onto every word. They closed-up around themselves like a ring of matrimony that is accepted too early in life.

There was a call for action: Something needed to be done! They lobbied to limit the flow of information. They promised to control the access to funds. They used the word "need" a lot when offering advice. They used the word "keep" a lot when describing natural functions.

Minor annoyances were becoming serious problems. They needed their rest, but could not get to sleep. It was sweets for diabetics, apnea for dreamers, the perception of a friend's disloyalty in the eyes of a narcissist...chaos in the realm of a designated quiet place. An ear to the wall could detect the vibrations of unwelcome sounds as they travel through ducts: It is the sound of the urine as it hits the water; it is the sound of the water as it moves through the pipes; it is the sound of blood as it moves through the body.

They were feeling emboldened by a popular vote that established the foothold for the new legislation; now, they could even wield this power on a microscopic level... They could form associations of neighbors to make everyone comply with their rules. Then, they could frame these rules for display in public buildings. First, they could tell them how to act. Next, they could tell them how to live. Soon, they would make them pay fees for these services rendered.

The rewriting of history was well underway. The theme of the story should be based upon suffering. The starring role shall be played by the victim. The plot involves a crime that is punished largely on the biases and prejudices of another. In fact, it does matter who one likes and dislikes! It is a truth that is found through emotional consensus. If thoughts are not in accordance with this consensus, they can be called thoughts of hate. If actions are instigated by these thoughts of hate, they can be called crimes of hate.

Support was procured in the public sector. Logically, they developed a special relationship with DIVINEAID, and contributed heavily to DIVINEAID's coffers. Still, DIVINEAID will only receive funds from them if they carry out their agenda: It is an agenda of abstinence. Do not tell the truth. Do not give the facts. Never differentiate between high-risk, low-risk and no-risk. Any word but "no" is considered to be destructive.

It is particularly important to focus upon sexuality. Remember, it is possible that everyone potentially harbors any number of diseases without knowing it. Theoretically, a person could infect anyone at any time... New information on this urgent subject is available at designated kiosks: This potential reality will be confronted by the formation of support groups for the survivors of sexual experience, isolated tiny chances of sloughed-off cells in satellite groups of the frustrated, never making connections.

Love could be tough. Expression is not free. Rules are rules: There is no other way. The conditions of love could now be amended; someone has to benefit from the rate of exchange. There is a concession of equality for the vow of commitment: Questionable words are subject to fines; touching is probably best avoided; kissing and hugging are personal threats. Codification is simple and easy: Close a dark curtain and walk into the booth.

Females shall hereafter be held by males in such high esteem that these males cannot talk to them, or even touch them, unless it is in reciprocation of an action that was initiated by a female. Of course, even this assumption of initiation shall be left to the discretion of the female. Finally, all of the laws that pertain to a female's personage shall always stress the primacy of the female over the male...as she is, in accordance, free to initiate any interchange that she chooses with said males...unless it involves prostitution: Prostitution shall always be declared illegal, as it disrupts the rules of commodification inherent in the sacred cycle.

Finally, the legal definition of sexual offense has expanded with the addition of these necessitous categories: when a male discusses his sexual attraction to a female for another person; when the female repeats the previously mentioned offense of the male to another woman, and she, too, feels offended; when a male discusses anything, whatsover, with a female who used to be a friend of the referenced female, but with whom she is now on bad terms; if a male declines any sexual advance perpetrated by a female; and, if a male discusses a female's physical appearance in anything but the most flattering terms.

It was time to advance the agenda in a most fitting way... A panel of guests were assembled by the talk-show with an injudicious discrepancy of ideological representation. Next, they were released upon the crowd to a roll-call of stomping and screaming. These are the movers and shakers of the foundation of the new democracy. It is where intelligence is equated with a rapidity of speech. It is where heads bob up-and-down with looks of concern.

The panel's appearance has been transformed to suggest a final authority...to evoke an earned sense of dignity. They have been coached to smile more than they frown; then, they are seated in a special position...only to be viewed from complimentary angles. It is a public relations of the deceptiveness of parallax, and where they identify with their audience...a feuding array of semi-circles in a wish-worn mirror.

A surprise guest is introduced like a cattle call through a chorus of boos: It is Minerva. She is possibly the most hated figure of the age, as she has committed its most heinous crime: She used to share the opinion of the public sentiment, but she has now changed her opinion. She tries to elaborate... The evolution of consciousness is contingent upon honesty with oneself. The expression of consciousness proceeds through phases of truth of experience. The racist must think racist thoughts. The homophobe must be homophobic. The xenophobe must live in a shell. It is part of the process.

Dishonesty with this process does not advance understanding: It muddies it. In fact, an intense emotion denied—such as hatred—will only be transferred to another person or group, however displaced. The policing of actions is a threat to experience. The policing of thoughts is a threat to acceptance. The desire to control is conducted through fear, as the fear is fanned by monitors of surveillance. Eventually, there would be no privacy at all. It would be a conflict of the absurd, like the enforcement of hand-washing when leaving the restroom.

Eventually, a society based upon political correctness will produce individuals whose fear of honesty with oneself---a fear of an honesty punished---will nurture such a lack of self-awareness that it will not be possible for them to know themselves. Moreover, individuals who do not know themselves cannot ever know what it is that truly brings them fulfillment: They will be forever doomed to a life of triviality.

An army of harpies and their retinue rise now in the front row—lock arms—and form two, moving, segmented lines, a pincer of movement on a freedom of speech. They are sporting a new hairstyle, which much of the audience has mimicked in adulation of their devotion to the cause. It is short, cropped and layered...and thought to embody the strong and decisive. In fact, it is severely terraced—thicker on top—with a clean ridge of 180 degrees at the tops of their necks. They are perfect prepuces covered in suppression, unconscious revelers in an officially outlawed priapic festival.

"We think that one should always wash his hands upon leaving a restroom."

CHAPTER SIX

The game had ended, but the obsession lived on. He returned to the oracle, but he didn't know why. The delusion had lifted, but he had a broken feeling. He wanted to heal it, but there was no diagnosis. It had no place to visit...no place to go. They avoided the subject that they could not release... There was an inappropriate necessity, uncomfortable and unnerving, like humor in the face of an unfolding calamity. The method of discourse was polite exchange, idle chatter over ravaged ruins: Their dove-tailing flight had flown into glass.

Thus began the time of his wandering. It played over and over again in his mind... Many days passed as the viewing continued. He needed to know. He was out there...pursuing exercises in futility—all kinds of fruitless endeavors—in a shabby state of disrepair. He was trying to make sense of it. He was trying to release what he had suppressed. He was a dutiful re-enactor.

One day, Prometheus left. It was mysterious, like the degree to which the persons around one who has suffered misfortune have been unconsciously complicit in the harmful sequence of events. He didn't want to care... Still, he waited for Prometheus. He returned to the oracle every day...waiting on the verge for a reason to leave, an enervated force at a status quo.

Then, his heart jerked-away like a poor piece of bait, stolen by surprise from a creeping depth. He could hear footsteps: They sounded like Prometheus'. He could feel his presence and he could smell his scent. He walked in his direction... He wondered if his movements seemed ambulatory or peripatetic. He wanted that definition, too. He felt excessive and over-worked, like preservation puzzles of unwilling nomads. He had taken on the look of a forensics specialist. The oracle didn't look the same, too.

Prometheus had planned the whole event. He was waiting at the oracle, as he knew his routines. He waited until the time that he passed. He sat in a proud corner, waiting there with pictures and mementos...detailed documentation of where he had been.

It seemed almost rehearsed. He even asked him if he could see them. He was like Bellerophon: He walked right up to it. Prometheus said nothing as he spread them onto the table. He had brought several tall stacks, and had lined them in order...levels of importance, hierarchies of intimacy. They were pictures of another, documents of love.

How could his perception have been so skewed? He had invested all of that energy... He had imagined all of those things. He had listened to his heart, but his heart had been wrong. His sustaining fields had flooded, as he sat there and listened to the sound of a sentinel. There is an economy of elegance in a primal scream: It is a murderous sound.

Prometheus seemed to experience some kind of an ecstasy. He could feel his own power. He had won the little game. Somehow, this moment was what he had needed. It filled in a milieu the niche that he craved. Then, it felt empty all over again. There was a panicky vigor, like inexperience. He had swallowed something sweet, but its container was dirty. A fruit-like knar of beauty protruded from his neck, and moved up-and-down. He sat there and stared into a distance... Everything had changed in a clipping of time.

He turned his back to Prometheus, and walked away. He walked to escape the sound of the sentinel. Thoughts raced in his head in sanguinous flush... He was questioning his strength. He was questioning his love. He wondered if he were capable of experiencing it. He wondered if he were even capable of knowing it.

It seemed that their energies were made for each other. Prometheus was more active in the beginning, and more passive in the end. He, himself, was more passive in the beginning and more active in the end. He had been searching for such a sacred cycle... Instead, he had found this strange oracle. He had come to believe that it was also deceptive. He had returned to it seeking answers, but they were encrypted in a symbolism of a syntax of knots. He felt all alone at a tainted wellspring, lost in a universe with a flawed design.

The sentinel was merciless. It was the sound of the chant, the pang from a distance. There was a urge to flee. It became louder and louder until it was almost upon him. It was crushing and disappointing, like the raised fist of a populace that will fight for a despot. "Crush! Crush! Crush! Crush!" He began to run to escape the pain; then, he descended into crisis. Soon, he collapsed from the stimulation.

There was a dullness. There was a numbness. Still, he could see more deeply than he had ever dreamed. His senses were heightened, but he could not yet see form. He could only see shapes in the yellowish-green. It dropped like virga before a tempest...as its weight increased until it hit ground, an unsure mist that falls in a fog.

He was lost, and his essence strayed. He looked with an automatic's motion upon his body's eyes... He saw a reflection. He saw a face. He did not even know whose it was: It was carved-out and hollow. He could not see his essence; he could only sense it, displaced...an empty vessel for white noise.

He had reached this place that his consciousness tried not to see. It was a place that his unconsciousness drew closer with every experience. He had reached an almost absolute empathy, but he retained one thing: He wanted his essence to return, but he would have to retrieve it.

He heard a voice... It arrived unfiltered by sensory experience. It bought no baggage from cultural tradition. It suffered no delusion from faith and superstition. It remained unscathed from personal trauma. It had no sound, but was crisp and clear. It bore an impassionate patience with a personal message. It came from a place of his highest consciousness.

"Gather and purge! Gather and purge!"

He could see the images as on digital display, set to a warped soundtrack of intermittent, sporadic sounds...a theme deconstructed through power-outages. He was viewing himself, inside of his body. He saw what he carried. He could feel what he believed...crashed into the wreckage of his own guilt and self-criticism: He landed on top of it.

There was the stuff that had kept him from moving... It clung like ugliness under the guise of honesty. It hardened in the cracks of his long-term goals. It turned to a solid when apprised of his abilities. It sneaked into his thoughts like an encroaching theocracy. It was layered like a compost of sentient toxicity. It was praised in the chant that he had never addressed.

It triggered a fulcrum, a memory of an event. There were two bedfellows, lying in a shelter, under an arbor. They had stayed-up late. It was their favorite time—that of their communion—when the creative wherewithal is at its peak. Night was still spreading her cloak; then they heard a chant.

It had the tenor of a trapped, wounded animal. There were pitiful squeals...disturbing, but familiar, like a family pet attacked in its yard. It was the sound of a knell, inciting a pall. It was horrendous, a perfect ploy with which to attack the empathic...unholy war-cries of victimization.

The walls were breached like a cluster of bombs: She said that she had caught them. They were guilty of the crime against nature, which—if left unpunished—could alter the heavens. First, they should never be allowed to see each other. Next, they should have to consider what others would think. Finally, they should never discuss it. She sent them home...as she sent it to the winds, and spread it over Earth; the original catechistic sermon for the co-dependency chorus.

"Shame! Shame! Shame! Shame! Shame! Shame!

"Shame! Shame! Shame! Shame! Shame! Shame!"

He was sitting in the lap of Earth when she arrived, still shouting. She wanted to talk to her in private, as she had something to conceal. He had a youthful zeal to listen... He wanted to hear what he was not supposed to hear...what was considered unmentionable. It aroused his curiosity, like unimaginable boundaries...a foghorn heard forty miles inland on a sunny day.

She knew that he was listening...as she grabbed Earth's hand, and put it in her own. She could only whisper of that which she had seen, though she could never erase the trauma. She had seen it with her own eyes...all of nature was frowning: The cozy lovebirds quit nesting; the little lambs quit milking; the playful pups quit sucking; the dutiful ants quit working.

She requested blessings upon Earth. Then she played upon her fears... She knew that Earth loved the young: The energy cycle that she had witnessed was not procreative; it would not produce her beloved children. They were a gift to her from the universe, and they are only procured by the ones who embody a large majority of either masculine or feminine energy, and agree to mingle…as each provides the other with what is lacking. It was the most common form of exchange: It was the seat of all power. It is what got us to this point.

These children were gifts to her…blessings from the universe, and they needed her protection. Indeed, they needed a place to be groomed—sacred places—where they could perform their procreative rituals. Teach them early and they would never forget. Shroud it in mystery. Create taboos to protect its sanctity. Christen it in name and proclaim it as a cycle. Make them form a circle to symbolize this cycle. Make them join hands…male-female-male-female.

Earth looked at him with a familiar paradox: She wanted him to be happy, but she wanted him to fit-in; she wanted him to be independent, but she wanted him by her side; she wanted him to be physically fit, but she wanted him to over-eat; she wanted him to spread his wings, but she wanted to clip them.

Night grabbed her tightly like a sister.

"Do it for the children!

"Do it for the children!

"Do it for the children!

"Do it for the children!"

They held each other as Night began to cry, repeating her refrain…gradually, relentlessly, until all of Earth began to shake. Then she appealed to her most maternal instinct, "You might never hear their little voices; you might never squeeze their tiny feet." At first, it registered as a tremor, but increased in forcefulness with the pattings of encouragement, and the volume of the refrain. Soon it was uncontrollable and incalculable, like the flapping of tails and fins in the muddy shoals at the end of the milky confluence, stacked on top of the entrails of the previous generations.

He felt devastated in the type of disappointment that springs from a horrible pit of inadequacy of deed. Earth begged him to attend the rituals—to wear the uniform—to participate as a willing inductee. He tried to fulfill her wishes, but he couldn't do it. It just didn't make sense to him. Soon, he was not even welcome... The social force of swirling motion had become a vicious flock, a circle of humiliation, a blanket of guilt presented with interrogation for the exclamation of self-criticism.

"SHAME! SHAME! SHAME! SHAME! SHAME! SHAME!

"SHAME! SHAME! SHAME! SHAME! SHAME! SHAME!"

He woke-up and convulsed...and emptied his stomach. There was a dizzying nausea, like a changing of the channels with a batting of the eyes...to a different time-zone in a seat facing backward. Then, with an even stranger sensation...his entire body rocked from a shedding of skin, a larval uprising for a psychological molting. He fell back asleep and continued his journey.

He saw microscopic creatures born under a sky with two heavenly bodies, as they were nourished and conditioned by the movements of their sun. This sun brought sustenance as it rose every day... Life was dependent upon its daily return, but the creatures evolved in a state of apprehension: The possibility that it would not return caused a separation anxiety.

There is a deep imprinting on the psyche, a jolt of panic to the primitive mind. An image is seen in the corner of the eye—almost dark—as its form is obscured. There is a recurring fiat on a singed surface of a time to leave. It is a coiled-up circle with an upraised head...slowly moving back-and-forth. It is a path across an inlet with a slippery bottom hiding spindly shapes. It is the whistling of a chasm of air under a falling tree.

His thoughts mixed with fear of the unexplained and unrealized, as they lent themselves to mythological subjects. He saw hardback illustrations of these creatures transmogrified between gastronomic fits. They were sentient, and had come to help him, moving in primal energies to fixed locales of ancient origin: They would be his guides.

He was no longer viewing his body from the inside: He was now in the space of the human psyche. Now he could feel the most primal fear that he had ever felt: The fear of dying. Suddenly, he was jolted from his body: Animals return to the dirt. There was a fear that he would go underground... He sensed that he was in a dark place, resembling a grave. Slowly, a light source became visible, warming his thoughts...allowing him to see. He was underground, but there was a way out... It was not a grave; it was only a tunnel...another pathway.

The light became stronger, like an archetypal hero. It was this sun—radiant like a god—the source of life. It seemed personal, like a friend, and true to its schedule. It had returned to lead him out of the tunnel, back to the tautology. Still, it disappeared every day. It was all or nothing... It was lightness; it was darkness; it was also vengeful... One could not stare at it without burning one's eyes. One could not look at it; one could not even know it. Still, its permanent disappearance would surely be destructive: It was a difficult taskmaster.

They developed creeds to quell this anxiety... Soon, they imagined the new gods, whose authors presented them with the ultimate absurdity: They had complex, ponderous minds... They could ponder eternity; they could ponder ontology, the essence of being. Unfortunately, they were not supposed to use them: They were given a new set of rules. Instead, they had to prove their faith; it was said that their survival depended on it. They had to show their faith in the return of the sun, and they had to prove it by believing in it blindly.

A passion play was always running to a packed congregation of a gene-pool of faith...whose characters would change, but would always be reborn in a celebration of this cult of return. This is where the signal would surface to search for responses to its call, sensing a faint response...muffled in the origins of the creation allegories. It would begin to stir, to descramble the subterfuge of the images scried in weightless pools...until it was silenced and buried in the footnotes of another's book of legacy.

There was a positive reinforcement of a biological imperative. The ones without it were hunted to death, making it unlikely they would survive to produce offspring...if they were ever interested. If they had produced offspring who did not display this imperative, then they, too, would likely be killed. There was a natural selection against a standard deviation... Rational thinking was considered disloyalty. Questioning minds were marginalized and punished. Exceptional minds were silenced and slaughtered.

Then, there arose the physical manifestations prominent in those regions that had selected strongly for blind faith. There were the square heads of smug configurations...the sunken, sheltered eyes under plowed parts of shocks of hair...most apparent when a conversation about natural disasters was engaged. It is the look of an arrogance of not trying to extend energy to reach a truth, or at least an understanding: It is like a birthright.

They would insist that their gods had sent these disasters because those individuals were not "good" devotees of their religion. There was no rational explanation that could be accepted to explain it: Their senses were now different. Their paradigm had shifted. They had natural defenses for irrational thoughts. Slowly, it began over the eyes as a film... This film would add consistency...until it was a glaze, thick and web-like. Finally, they had achieved the physical protection to keep them from seeing... Their ignorance was now complete, literally, a blind faith.

• • •

Thank you, Dears, thank you. Now, it is my delight to introduce to you the return of a legend...here to recite a poem for the epoch...

• • •

CHAPTER SEVEN

Humanity continues to gather, unaware of its seats. Still, they are performing some kind of a theme music, a quotidian ritual. It is only called 'music' because they are unconscious of their roles. If they were...it would be called theatre. Thank goodness that they are not, Dear.

"They have developed a machine which provides unlimited access to the arts, sciences and an unconstructed historical record. One can merely introduce a word or a phrase, and immediately engage in intellectual dialogue. One can blithely go in whatever direction about which one is curious, like the best kind of vacation. This enriching option is now at their fingertips; yet, they are not interested.

"They are worried about appearances, and checking their faces. They are eating on the lawn, and sitting on blankets. They are talking about feelings, but have largely displaced them. They pour beverages from bottles and clank their glasses. They are talking into devices and checking their watches. They have mechanized production, but no time for themselves... They are animals tagged for another's control...in a hurry to go home and do nothing at all...

"Hmmm... As above so below... It has always been the same...until now! Put both of your hands on your hats, Dears... It is time to announce the first glimpse of the alternative stage! Come to mother! We are over here... somewhere between tolerance and acceptance. Come to mother...my lovely diaspora, my hidden jewels...

"... And you, with the cleft chin... Where have I seen you? Was it with Theocritus, as the inspiration for one of his idylls? Well, I'm not looking for a Hylas with hair of gold! ...And you? Weren't you that fey reference in one of Shakespeare's sonnets? 'Where the bee sucketh, there suck I'...? Or, was it you who were scuttling about in some Forest of Arden? ...And you, Dear... over there...weren't you filling Rumi's carafe with wine as he asked you to contemplate the moving image as the arrow of love that penetrated his target in a game of bellomancy, or were you the muscled Hyacinthus teasing the smitten Apollo with your accuracy? Yes, now I recall... You were enjoying the 'manly love of comrades' with Whitman one night in the dunes of Provincetown for the songs of Calamus.

"...And you... Not you again, Dear! What do I have to do to prove to you that I am not interested? I have told you countless times that... What? Let me see you again? Oh! Excuse me. I've mistaken you for someone else... At least I made you blush. It is my theory that blushing is tangible proof of the evolution of consciousness, represented incorporeally: One cannot hide his true emotions from another, unless, that is...he has learned to conceal them.

"These shackles that they have placed upon enlightened experience are threatening our augury. It is imperative that we recollect our thoughts and concentrate on voice. Come with me as I take you to some of my favorite places for character study. Remember, Dear, the best places never have a cover charge, while the main entrance is in the rear. One more thing... don't open the side doors, or you might let the nighttime out.

"Follow me down this hallway..."

A family of three is particularly noisy as they arrive from inside of an elevator as its sticky doors close sluggishly like a thick, blood sugar. They struggle up the rampart toward the unhealthful food that is dispensed from the machines, as an obese little girl runs up ahead and presses her nose against the viewing window; then, she jumps up-and-down, out-of-breath.

"Mama! Mama! I want a ding-dong! I want a ding-dong!"

The mother puts a stubby hand out in front of a forearm, which carries several plastic grocery bags lined-up to her elbow—and to the sleeves—of a tee shirt that she wears...which is emblazoned with a crafty but sweet cartoon character whom she somehow resembles. It is a symbolic presupposition: Her heaviness will be duly noted by a tactless society of consumers, but it will embrace her for participating in it.

She waves her hand around...

"You cain't have no ding-dong! You've already had onced already today!"

"Oh, Mama! I want a ding-dong! I want a ding-dong!"

Her boyfriend, who does not look like the consanguineous father of the child, walks behind them. It is his time to contribute to the family...as he tugs on his crotch.

"I've got your ding-dong right here, hehehe........."

This hallway leads into another room, where Pan's train have taken the stage... Fire-eaters are writhing to the sounds of percussion. Torches are lit from soft, metal sculptures. The sculptures are shaped like pistols and stamens. Flames shoot outward from the tips of their organs... Everyone glistens in oil-based lubricants as a tall drag-queen waves her hands where she sits on a swing that hangs from a tree that edges a path, just like in a painting. A swarthy attendant walks past in a costume that is scented in sweat from actual exertion...embodying a fantasy, a charioteer. Silenus rides up on a threadbare mule...

He dismounts the animal and crouches onto the ground, unpacking a pipe that he carries in a satchel. It smells ripe and jellied, like Persian apples in an earthen barrel. He expectorates seed hulls in the attendant's direction, as hashish is available in return for some favors...while he talks in a way like he's coaxing a monkey.

"Hey! Hey! Te-te-te-te. Come!"

He nods to reaffirm his intent amongst chittering sounds and a double winking of the eye. There is a flicking of the hulls as he reaches for his hand with a tickling of the palm... It is a code of discretion, learned by initiates, like a blue-light hung from a back-door at night. He molds his thumb and index finger into a rounded "O", and moves them up-and-down over the index finger of the young attendant. Some symbols are easy to crack...

Another stage is waiting—and another hallway—long and carpeted, whose wall is lined with old convention chairs.

"Alright, Dears...grab a hat, choose a role. What mask will you be wearing?"

Hushed voices lend support to a still of smoke, body fluids and stains from a roof that leaks onto old fabric. A joyful bell sounds as if from below a little lamb, eliciting a Pavlovian response from persons sitting in the lobby...alerting them that a new customer has arrived. There, Mother Goose has been waiting all day with his train for the fruits of their day labor. In fact, he has stayed-up all night, and was waiting at the front door when it opened.

"Stay away from The Slurper, Hunny! I wouldn't have believed it unless I had seen it for myself!"

Here he comes, dressed in the unassuming way of youthful, casual dress...the well-heeled background of pre-professional tradition. He pays his fee of admittance, and turns to the stairwell...which he descends gracefully. Slowly, he proceeds to lift his arms to his chest, higher with each exertion, as he hums a trill of rambling, minor chords...all of the way to the end of the hallway...and into the tearoom.

"He'll stay in there all night, Hunny, unless The Crab chases him out.

The Crab is busy in his den, or his stall, keeping it tidy with a fastidious knowledge of tearoom etiquette. There, he waits for the new customers to arrive, intermittently walking over to his glory-hole opening and peering through to the next stall. Occasionally, he will remove a cutting-tool from his pocket to chip away at its circumference. Next, he will take a piece of cardboard and smooth the edges...forever refining the art of customer service.

The door slams open with on-shore abandon as The Soldier marches in wearing green fatigues and spit-cleaned boots. He has learned well to serve his country; now, he is ready to serve the crowd. He lodges into the stall, adjacent to The Crab's, who watches with anticipatory clitter-clatter, as he sporadically pokes his fingers through the hole, and winces.

The Soldier has a logistical problem that has aroused everyone's curiosity: His fatigues have gotten stuck halfway down his well-formed buttocks. Still, there are offers of help from all over the tearoom... Here comes The Retiree from across the room... He is a marvel of determination—with two bad hips and a walking stick—as he hugs the walls and bounces off of corners like a spinning top. One night he collapsed from the exertion of servicing so many men that the management thought that he was dead. They even called the police, who called his wife...to identify him. Incidentally, his dentures were never found.

This job will require the expertise of The Engineer, however...who is first in line. Here, he specializes in dilemmas involving high summits and tight trousers... Of course, his instructions are imperative, and must be followed meticulously: The Soldier will have to agree to his exact specifications. First, he must lay his hands upon the back wall of the stall. Next, he must relax his buttocks...so that they can receive a slap from a durable, all-weather metal ruler. Finally, when they flinch to just the right degree, he will reach up and yank them to the ground... as the keys on his belt-loop jingle-jangle. Of course, they have almost perfected this technique, as they meet in this stall every Thursday night at this time.

The Athlete springs past them and positions himself onto his haunches, in front of The Batter, i.e., The Soldier, as he opens his mouth and moves it back-and-forth.

"Jus lemme catch it!"

The tearoom is now quite crowded... The Businessman arrives during his lunch-break to check his watch. He is on a busy schedule, and he will have to meet clients in half an hour. The Romantic stands on the top of the seat of the commode in the opposite stall, as he peers down at The Soldier as if he is perusing a profile from a personal's column. He takes his right hand and positions it outside the top button of his shirt as he wiggles his curled-up fingers in the direction of each new arrival, while opening his eyes unnaturally for emphasis.

"Girl!"

The Denier stands behind him—with a full view—as he repeats what he says every night with a shrieking, sliding countenance. Incidentally, he is wearing a pin on his lapel that proclaims, "I voted!" Indeed, he voted, as he always does... for the candidate that would hang him for his preference.

"This is the first time that I've done this! Honest! I've never done this before!"

The Engineer collapses onto The Soldier, ruler onto canteen, as The Slurper puts his hands behind his back, accentuating a slightly bowed mien...and makes his move. He taps The Engineer on the shoulder...

"Do you have something for me?"

The Engineer slowly unrolls it, and hands it to him.

He smiles, and takes his donation...as he lifts it up to the light in an examination of textural vitality. Then, he turns it up as the bottom of his tongue looks like a string-bean in a bag.

"SLLLRRRPPP!"

"I told you to stay away...she's a sick queen, Hunny!"

A series of bows to the crowd signals a change of theme...

"Thank you, Dears, thank you. Now, it is my delight to introduce to you the return of a legend...here to recite a poem for the epoch. It will be presented in three acts throughout the reverie, each of which has been choreographed under my direction. I present to you now, after ages of censorship...the first act of 'A Bouquet of Exotica,' entitled 'Meme-Pool'"

He disappears as the stage is black and the disruptions abate. A mellotron chorus begins as a whisper, slowly gaining strength as it thrives, growing unconcerned with criticism. Gradually, a scene emerges, presented to the eyes like through cones at a full eclipse, until peering as through vertical beads onto a new world appearing through the strands of a breaching pupa.

There is a crashing bass-line. Glitter falls through fog-bank lighting, illuminating vessels adorned with geometric renderings of stylized nature, like the precursors of modernism at the palace of Knossis, or the delicate abstraction of the Moche line. Wine-colored tufts of grass-fronds hide Pre-Raphaelite eyes telling telescopic secrets by Elizabethan symbols of mystic navigation.

Strobe lights chase a pheremonal scent of a divine/man/beast through thrones of peacocks on feathery perches, with multiple voice-loops. It is a different take of a saucy Atalanta, dangling a chain for a phlegmatic crowd, reciting lyrics of rebellion like runaway adolescents while sipping champagne.

"Prancing barefooted under a velvet gown

"In a domed arboretum

"Like the sisters of Hesperides...

"Where seasonal flowers with hybridized genes

"Hang from stripper-pole trees

"Henna-pressed hair that moves in a breeze

"Of Arabesque design

"While Cleopatra eye-liner lends noblesse-oblige

"Like tutus for suburbia

"And absynthe for mead

"With symbols of plentitude like vitamin D

"From a disk of the sun

"In a diadem of beads..."

Falsetto squeals crash into cymbals with a gesture to the audience like a hidden nymph with a lily in her ear, or a flick of the wrist like the hand of Ophelia, just breaking the water. He turns his head slightly off-scale like a being who sees a faintness from a moving bright light that is shown in its direction from another time.

"Like a roiling boil of a Chaldean whore

"Either or not! Is his chant d'amour

"He scoffs at the means to possess the ability

"Through an excess of glamour

"And a spoof of vanity

"Fists in the air to mock the pomposity!

"A bouquet of exotica with a red-hot poker.

"Thus, as refinement freed from the symbols of status

"He cringes when told of adoring masses

"As from the arms of a stifling lover...

"An awakening conscience!

"Of unexpressed elements at their most expressive

"Like the censored object of Narcissus' lust

"And the documents burned of a chronicled life

"The unwilling prototype of canonization

"And the deification

"Of Antinus

"Uprooted, so deep was the extirpation;

"Or, the identity of the loin-clothed youth

"A character from the mystery schools

"In holy irony, never understood

"Who shed his clothes at Bethany

"As an eschatological hide-and-go-seek

"A sublimated insurrection.

"But divine inspiration was carried in breath

"And knowledge of self shines through holes of glory

"Viewed from down upon knees

"Of priests, sanctified by preserving the stories

"By sharing the wisdom, stored in the seed;

"And the halls of the churches are now museums

"Whose walls are adorned

"With the visage of beauty

"Artifice, transformed as a natural scheme

"Restoring the temples extirpated by fear

"Each to his ability, in praise of experience

"And these prisons of spirit are finally freed."

There is an abrupt change of arrangement. He disappears into a sylvan scene, an urbane bohemian's foray into the country through translucent veils, suspended from branches. He is a lute-playing dandy who hears a sound from waist-high weeds...whose blooms reach to the bottom of his coat, tickling his tights. A cygnet arrives from beneath a dark bough to the ripples of sunlight in an active pool as repeating arpeggios of multi-tracked voices, swaddled in ancient themes, are reversed and repeated and reunited.

"Cascades of curls like lavender roses

"For handmaids of Venus

"As they ready a bath of citrus and tonic

"With buttercup gauze or a triplicate head

"In the lap of the goddess

"Who sighs like the whispers of oaks

"In a bed of ferns.

"Aeolian harps and averted stares

"In openings of forests

"Of dancing faeries in little balls of light

"In ongoing orgies, graceful as artists

"Transform their lives preparing to open

"As dandelion tufts to a factory of spirals

"Where bird-faced beings with dragonfly wings

"And marmoreal spines support miniature bodies

"Like tiny cetaceans with beams of buttocks

"And hats of foxgloves on druidic figurines

"Follow their passions through an aural dream

"A performance piece in mixed-media

"For a band of synesthetes tasting the sound

"Of their deepest voices

"Before absconding the dawn for a full day of rest

"And make deosil shapes from widdershins."

An operatic chorus runs onto the stage anticipating movements in an interstitial dance within the spaces between the beats, wearing lacquered masks that are stained to an ochre by breath-taking pollen that falls from pods that twirl as they fall from the sky like cultivating fertile crescents. His back is turned to the crowd as his hands move slowly upward to the highest point that is reachable when extended, and then stop. A white light penetrates his crenellated sleeves which form a full eclipse from his waist to his shoulder. Eight cascading rays shine through the spaces of his fingers, into infinity, a focusing of parting glances, renewing his body through the creative wherewithal, like dreaming for sleeping.

> "Heretofore
>
> "Sang the spirits of the dandies!
>
> "Johnny-jump-up
>
> "Tickle-my-fancy
>
> "Cull-me-to-you
>
> "Kiss-him-in-the-pantry
>
> "Thereupon
>
> "We shall christen thee a pansy!"

• • •

They are living next to the schools:
The predators are everywhere.

• • •

CHAPTER EIGHT

We have gathered here today to discuss humanity; we have convened to show our concern. It is now impossible not to see them as they truly are... Just look at them, Dear. Here are the chosen. Here are the newly chosen... Everywhere are the elected. There are the sisters... There are the brothers.

"It is not as if there were not advances... They had overcome some real cultural barriers: The world's poor were willing to work for a very low wage. They experienced innovations in technologies: They viewed images of slaughter in sold-out cinemas. There was a comingling of peoples, and a flourishing of their arts: A popular culture grew.

"At least, there was novelty. Novelty, however, does not imply appreciation... Empty trends fed upon trends. Silly fads fed upon fads. Cultural impresarios churned-out products as popularity was defined by one's means to consume. These consumers were desperate to define themselves, and operators were available to take their calls.

"Still, an inexorable evidentiality was stalking them: Mathematics was not on their side. Most of the cultures had now been discovered, while most of their features had now been shared. Unique and original ways to combine them were diminishing in number: All of the melodies had already been sung. Finally, it really was the same old song, Dear. The supply of novelty could not meet the demand of insecurity inherent in this awareness. The pace of cultural change slowed as attention spans dropped...

"Of course, they wanted to see their bland lives validated by easy improvisation: Thus, they would cannibalize their previous accomplishments... Older works were redone without the power of the originals as art and consumption merged in the banality of obsolescence. Ironically, the creative void that was left through this cruel division provided the perfect surface on which they would write their epitaph in a culture of nostalgia.

"They have organized the perfect forum in which to celebrate this lack of passion: the community arts festival. Here they wait for the weekends to leave their enclaves in the hinterlands to peruse vendor's markets and eat over-priced food that is thought to be exotic, but returns every year. There is such a lack of vitality that one cannot tell that there is an event at all, until one arrives at this oasis...where art is safe, and music cannot be louder than noise ordinances allow. They are uninteresting allegories for a humorless society, acknowledging each other as clowns on their way to a staged event, but spotted in public: They are acknowledging their cuteness.

"Dear, I just deplore a sad parade..."

* *

The music of humanity only gets louder... It is sung now in strained exhilaration and empty stances, in the voices of caricatures of persons of interest of ages past. It is a sad device, providing a sense of reflection where no reflection is present: It is the hiding place of the covert narrators. It is the strange circumstance where the people who have acquired the means to develop themselves have no desire to do so... They sing to an audience of idle minds, scanning the ether for stressful interludes.

It is a swindle of identity by a skewing of a purpose. It is the arrival of the occasionally seen relatives at the house of a wealthy kinsperson—who is in his final days—while making a spectacle of their availability: They will try to discredit the ones who have always been available. It is the celebrating of a holiday from a bordering country that does not, in fact, celebrate it: It is a commercial bonanza, using little fabrications of collective disinterest in the cultural history of others. It is a handbook distributed by an occupying military force explaining the cultural habits of the conquered, but ancient people, in succinct rows of color-coded diagrams of "useful" knowledge: It will be studied so that they can be slaughtered in a less dangerous way.

It doesn't really matter... The supplies are dwindling; there is an underlying panic. Their behavior is problematic when the supplies are plentiful... It is a problem for all when they are limited. Still, they don't want to know... The doors will open at five a.m. The parking lot is already filling up... They want bigger cars for smaller spaces. They demand more than one space for their bigger cars. The stores will stay open until everything is sold. Fights are breaking-out for the final, blind grab.

The entertainment monitors are running in a row on an aisle in the store, as the talk show begins. There is a blotched face on a massive screen, overlooking the audience...a demagogue with special interests. The emcee is talking to the face: They have made peace. His is a voice of the patriarchy. Hers is a voice of the matriarchy. They are ready for rapprochement, as ownership and control walk hand-in-hand.

There is a "y" in the wherefore, as he is making his case...angry and itchy, while pointing a finger. There should be no discussion... He is promoting her insecurity by promoting her fear... She needs his protection. She should do it for the children. She should do it for the youths. The streets are now crawling with persons who want to hurt them... They are going to the churches. They are living next to the schools: The predators are everywhere.

The sacred cycle is under attack! Forces are gathering to corrupt its instruction in what could only be described as a war of the cultures. These forces have now been identified: It is the common enemy. In fact, they are apostates... They used to hide, but now, they are flaunting. These are the men who do not need their manhood. These are the women who do not need to enable them. They are partaking in uncommon energy exchanges, like an egg-fusion.

These exchanges are historically associated with something else: Aestheticism. Aestheticism could be discouraged in a compliant society by an association with elitism; in fact, it should not be called elitism: It should be called affectation. Ironically, it is an affectation that is elitist...but somehow pan-cultural. It is infinitely threatening, as its appreciation can easily cross cultural barriers, like an innate Esperanto.

It is vital that it be eviscerated from daily activities. It should never surface in everyday speech. The homogenized way is the most compliant way... If it is heard, it should be ridiculed: Deepest voices are only found in intimidating tones! Speak in the present tense, but do not live in the present. News should be seen as a form of entertainment. Entertainment should be provided by reactionary hosts. Stigma is attached to language and art. Reading is viewed as being worthy of suspicion. Writing is thought to be suspicion confirmed. Refinement is the ultimate result of this process. Punishment is encouraged if it affects one's speech. It is clearly a threat to display sophistication: Aesthetics is held for these acts of sedition.

The blotched face concludes his argument to the crowd on behalf of suppression: He has decided to invoke his religion. Now, he is a victim; in fact, they are causing him pain. The apostates are causing him pain by stating their truth... It is that upsetting to him. Of course, it could be called a crime of hate. It is important for them to understand that their lives must be controlled in order to ensure their eternal happiness: It is only the ultimate swindle.

He utters an impromptu closing statement.

"We must think of it as a game... We are in this game to win it. Let me be clear: It is a mandate. There are fine, young men on our side... They need to know that we are behind them. We must commit ourselves, long and hard, to this mandate

* *

The final war was underway with one obsession: mass destruction. They had grown socially desperate while seeking affinity groups, while, as individuals, they grew more opportunistic. They were like the special forces of the military: adjust and adapt, but only enough to accomplish a campaign that is not of their making.

Still, it was not happening... The countries had changed; the timeframes were wrong: Now, they would have to make it happen. They would fulfill it, and they would have to hurry... There were significant dates and markers for this planned apocalypse... They founded ersatz versions of long-forgotten nations. They had satellites in the sky, but talked of armies on horseback. There would soon arise the dueling prophets from the different traditions...as the victorious prophet would make everyone believe in him—might is right—encouraged in force by an emotional consensus.

It happened during the time of the greatest freedom... A reactionary base was mapped and staked who were wary of talking of proclivities and bell-curves. They wanted the return of easy dichotomies, but they could only move forward by going back to happy days. These were days spent with males and females, black or white, wearing either pants or skirts, appropriately, acting rightly or wrongly.

There was a tour de force, and the public was ready! A movie was made that moved the culture...a vision of the future—a vision of war—that was comfortably familiar. The warriors were like cowboys and Indians, whose guns and horses had been traded for lasers and spaceships. It was a refocusing of an epic charade, a battle of good versus evil...a high-jacking by guerilla fighters against the evolution of consciousness.

A homeland was attacked... They gave up their rights for a guarantee of protection. They demanded visual celebrations of national holidays. Flags and banners should wave in the street as the ancient agreement could now be renewed: The men leave on foot and the women stand beside them; the men leave on beast, and the women stand beside them; the men leave on machine, and the women stand beside them.

The sacred cycle needs its fuel. There are promises to return, and tearful goodbyes. The men will go to claim their prizes... The women will wait for their prizes returned... Manhood's economy is written in code: It is the transaction that undergirds the commodity and the currency. It has to be won, and it has to be notarized. Only the women are granted a license. The payment is only accepted in blood. Chivalry seals it like a flag on a tomb whose contents are no longer allowed to be viewed by the public.

It had its own kind of rhythm... The men on the top would choose their enemies. The men at the bottom would follow their orders. The possession of women was the greatest commodity, while the killing of man was the preferred currency. Its enforcement was said to be the burden of man: They created the mythos of the slaughter of the bull.

One day it changed... They developed machines to aid in efficiency. They could fly high above the clouds, high above their enemies. They could view them in retreat; they could view them in surrender. Still, there was one obvious question: Why not just build another tall monument of marble at the base of a canal...one with an eponymous title? It didn't matter... They were eager to shoot. They were eager to kill. They drew lines in the sand, as the dog-fight became a turkey-shoot under a sky lit with fireworks.

They felt guilt about not having proved their manhood in the traditional way...to give them the respect that their fathers never gave them. They became naive and childlike with skills of comprehension. They called the previous generation the greatest of all, though it left little for them. Clearly, they were different from their fathers in one important way: They were efficient swindlers. They would defend the irrational in the face of evidence to the contrary. They would defend it even when it was not in their best interest.

The worst were the ones who had never gone to war. They felt that they should fight, but had not created the opportunity. They wanted the spoils, but did not go and get them. They needed their manhood, but had not seized the chance. They had taken no prizes, and they had brought nothing home. Of course, someone had to pay for this missed opportunity: Others could be sent to prove their manhood by proxy. They became overly zealous of services rendered. They discussed the killing of civilians as moral equivalency. Casualties in conflict could not be avoided... Someone must pay for their manhood unearned.

* *

The ceremony is about to begin as the closed coffins are prepared to be carried on the street, single file. Thus begins this manipulation of the depersonalization of battle. The general public is now discouraged from making the palpable connection of death with a familiar face. Next, all heads are asked to bow as a national anthem is sung, embracing a union of divine will with national pride. Strangely, it is a song that was stolen from the repertory of the previous ruling empire, whereupon—after a successful rebellion, many years previous—its words and imagery were replaced with new words and imagery.

The new union of necessity has reverted to using a term of identification that has not been common since the inception of the nation, of a type which denotes a fact of division from a fear of collapse, invoking the myth of foundation. There is no room for error in this divisive politics: One is either a patriot, or one is not.

They are praising the fallen, faceless soldiers as preservers of society... as the mercenaries of necessity that should be immune to criticism, even if they are not acting in self-defense... nothing but mere vessels of the greater will, soldiers of fortune for the mystical cause. Conversely, now that the enemies have been named, their real names can be corrupted to sound like evil characters or places from the myth of foundation. It is the ironic final act of depersonalizing them by personalizing their demonization. Finally, they can be killed without the slightest care: It will be a cleansing.

Here play the battles for ownership and control in this sacred cycle... One sex oppresses the other sex until the suppressed sex clamors for equal rights. Gradually, this hitherto oppressed sex will begin to gain some comparative measure of equality. Predictably, it shall soon begin to seek a remuneration for its past oppression, in whose pursuit shall be established the basis for justification of special rights. Eventually, they will procure these special rights, angering the newly oppressed sex, and triggering the renewal of this conflict in a similar sequence of events. There is, however, the transitory resolution in the demonization of those whose subjugation might prove sufficiently profitable and socially galvanizing to sustain the current cycle, or of those who do not participate in it... as even the well-meaning minds on both sides are ultimately corrupted by a union of reactionary conservatism, deluded by a belief in their own compassion.

The talk-show resumes with a discussion of an economy. It is unprecedented, and it is failing. In fact, there will soon be nothing left. There will be nothing to leave to the children. The wealth of the past has been exhausted. The wealth of the present has been squandered. The wealth of the future has already been leveraged. The old voodoo has lost its mojo: There are no more rabbits to pull out of the hat. The much weaker nations have already been invaded to rob them of their natural resources...to restructure capital. Yet, an error of judgment adversely effected this outcome: They fought back. The time has come to claim the resources of the common enemy at home. Besides, they do not deserve them. They are like aliens among us.

The harpies storm the stage—each waving a flag—and incite the crowd to fight them... to reclaim what is rightfully theirs. Minerva is called to the dais amidst the obligatory boos of anticipatory negation. A new feature has been added, however: The opinions of this impartial audience are simultaneously being recorded electronically, and immediately displayed to measure the degree of anger that they feel upon hearing each word that is spoken... It is a willful of collision of flesh upon plastic, mind upon icon, a feedback cycle of hysteria for a box filling with trapped, noxious vapors.

They extol the crowd to reclaim the boundaries, as they parrot a partisan timeline, a processional calendar: First, seal the border; second, secure the homeland; third, interrogate and intern the guilty; fourth, seize their assets. The crowd responds by waving thousands of tiny, synthetic flags, while dressed in the colors associated with the proclaimed virtues of the homeland.

"Seal the border!"

"Seal the border!"

"Seal the border!"

Minerva arrives onto the dais, as a question assails her from the hostile crowd.

"Are you a patriot?"

She pauses for a moment, startled in this rare moment of a necessitous, binary morality and intellectual evidentiality. She has only two personally acceptable choices: Be silent or speak her truth.

The audience member reiterates his demand.

"Are you a patriot...yes or no?"

She begins...

"This wasn't the way that it was supposed to be... If humanity is to evolve in a positive way, it will likely be achieved through world-wide cooperation...a confederation of different cultures, wherein is engendered a respect for these different identities. It will be a world without borders, with only one currency, where each individual shall travel freely throughout. It will have to begin with the individual, as one must take responsibility for his or her actions. It is like the ethos of a self-help group for personal recovery: The first step is to become conscious of the process.

The crowd erupts again...

"Secure the homeland!"

"Secure the homeland!"

"Secure the homeland!"

One of the harpies holds aloft a copy of a "statement" that has been attributed to her. In fact, it is a poem. She waves it in front of her face and shouts its title to the assemblage, "A RAPE OF EXCHANGE..." Then, she stands directly in front of her, demanding that she authenticate it, and claim or deny its authorship. Minerva nods her acknowledgement. Next, she demands that she denounce it as being unpatriotic. Minerva refuses. Now, she demands that she read it to the crowd...

I was never so young as the young men who fight

For their country at war when their country is wrong

With an opened account in the balance of man

Thus invested for women in a family of blood

Where the killing of men is a badge of honor
Passed through fingers of soldiers on decks of cards
These prizes for games played with pictures of hunted:
A bounty of allegiance is the young man's reward!

While collecting these badges of service to country
Their accomplices say to leave them alone
"They are only fighting an old man's war;
The wealth of man is the sacrifice of the young"

As these opened accounts are extended in duty
From the families of brothers of victims they felled
They are shielded from cries of their killing for hire
For complicity requires that they think for themselves

These lessons of history…devolved into blood-baths
And abandoned in fields by reconnaissance of poison
Are returned to their country in caskets unopened
Like the muted discussions of unquestioning warriors.

Thus their balance is lost in these cycles of violence

The exchange of manhood is the lifeblood of man

As their badges return to their families of blood:

A collection of parts for another's sum.

The crowd erupts with the mocked, vociferous boos of a staged response to a greatest outrage: ugly, stacked facial features of twisted lips, open mouths and raised eyebrows angling for a camera. Thus sings this chorus of clarity to which Minerva is expelled from the talk-show...high-minded arias silenced by four chords and a lack of skill by a calamitous, spewing sea whose contents are dislodged by storms and released with a corrosive acidity of painful simplicity.

A refined sense of clarity issues forth from this truth of experience, this violent rejection, providing the numbness of release for the moral responsibility of others, a pragmatic acknowledgement of the obvious. She knows now that this humanity may never be capable of receiving the help that she had so desperately wanted to provide, and she knows that it is not her responsibility to provide it. In fact, if she were to pull them out from a ditch, they would probably only accuse her of having thrown them into it. There is, however, one element in common to the most joyous societies that she has known, where like-minded individuals come together to celebrate their individual expression, where everything is optional, including clothes...and nothing is stressed, except, perhaps, the encouragement of others' dreams...where much of life really is like a parade.

It is here that she arrives at the ironic realization: The evolution of social consciousness will require the individual separation of the conscious ones from the unconscious others. It is only the difference between selfishness and self-interest... Now, it is time to proclaim a new family that shall form the foundation of this peaceful society... where the feminine is still nurturing...but more rational, and the masculine is still experiential...but more empathic. It is time to lead them to the new stage.

• • •

Sometimes the signals are even mixed, inciting a fear that they might secretly be that which they had sought to demonize.

• • •

CHAPTER NINE

There is an exhibition at the arts festival, a group show in a gallery. He recognizes its references, but somehow, does not understand its arrangement. There is an attempt at narrative. There are diagrams and charts and illustrations...artistic representations of economic interests, a bartering economy based upon unshared needs.

It is a blow-job for a fur coat. It is a fresh apple pie for a warm embrace. It is a lifetime of housework for cunnilingus. There are clear images with confusing goals, beautiful pictures with a meaningless background. There are clear goals with warring players. There are interesting theories that suddenly stop, stymied by an arrested development. There is a rage at the injustice of this conflict of interest. There is an embracing of the lyrical and quotidian as an answer to this rage.

It is an understanding of space with no place to put it. There are rules of a mating-game that have been covered with a fixing element, halting any hope of progress, palimpsests of images and words, superimposed upon others. Strangely, it reminded him of the notice that had arrived... It was neatly packaged, an insert in an envelope, swathed in a scent associated with renewal...addressed to him. A date was written in a formal font, an announcement of a wedding, a request for his presence.

An image of a couple was highlighted in the center of the page. Prometheus was holding a young lady in a playful embrace. Still, there was a tension. She was leaning back as if she were about to fall. He was reaching behind her, catching her, supporting her back, unswayed. She was holding him for support, hair flying off of shoulders, into a breeze. They were posed with pressed cheeks, facing the viewer, looking forward into a life together, smiles in a measured space shared with other images and words of a similar theme.

He felt disconnected from Prometheus, with no remorse. Now, it felt too foreign; he didn't even care. He no longer needed to try to walk in his path. The game that had ended no longer mattered... He just sat there and stared into a distance of disinteresting images of their lives, graduated semiotics of disassociation, fading-out like warning signs seen only with hindsight in the alienating quiet of feeling oneself removed from mutual plans.

It is an unnatural art where a natural antagonism obscures the esthetic. It is a narrative for a borderline expression, an outward portrayal of an inner dialogue of the sacred cycle in decay. Its modus operandi is one of polemics, where incompatible interests meet to confirm a contract...rife with the tedium of a business agreement. There is a proliferation of imagery, text, and narrative critiqued by its own bureaucracy, whose ancillary functions are predicated upon acquisition and accumulation, where an allegiance to its politics bequeaths money and status.

There is one overriding goal: the possession of credentials to promote a career. It is what happens when art is forced to choose a side... The ones who are most easily groomed by a bureaucracy, and who know how to work within it, are the most celebrated. The framework is not to be questioned, but the discussion of the less significant finer points is encouraged...in fact, it is actively pursued. It represents the veneer of a fertile discourse of ideas, a culture of self-serving disputation and partisanship that is said to be meritorious.

It is work that bears a forced intellectualism, a brainstorming that is born of deadlines, leaving little room for the inspiration and complexity that are born of patience. Still, subtlety can be useful... Works can be sponsored by corporations and political organizations if their agendas are suggested. Grants and endowments are awarded to the ones who learn to weave these suggestions into their craft. It is a necessary tactic, because a financial trail should not be hidden, but it should not be obvious. Eventually, the definition of mastery is redefined as an allegiance expressed by cunning and gimmickry, requiring a huge volume of work.

It is the incorporation of the fine arts into a subset of the social sciences, a pastiche of psychology, sociology, anthropology, and political science. It is where a discourse of complex ideas is limited by the medium...as an understanding of beauty is replaced by expediency, and the routes of visibility are contingent upon economics. Thus, the canvasses on the wall are like pages of a text, figures on a screen, accompanied by graphics for a biased report.

The worst ones are laudatory, equaling propaganda. The best ones are one-punch jokes, political cartoons. They are captured in a brief moment of irony or cynicism, a personal time-line of possessions or images connoting socio-economic status, sexual, ethnic and racial identities. It is the portrayal of objectification with actual objects. It is like bemoaning an illiteracy of geography by using a guiding system.

Still, there is an abstruseness that denies the subject, a muted undercurrent of resentment. Somewhere in the pictorial of meaning...through the montage of feeling for a short-term impact, is a vicarious thrill, like second-hand smoke. It is a displaced anger that comes from a forced political correctness, the unconscious knowledge that one does not feel the way that one would like to feel.

Here is found the appropriate vessel for the hidden, covert narrators: their own animation. It is a transformation of self-perception for ones who have no foundation for their own maturation. Now, in the shape of zoomorphic cut-outs, they can rejoin the narrative in a dense, pressed-together protean landscape where they can reference the difficult issues, while remaining unexposed.

****

It was a system in the land called Peril where there is a fear that things are no longer working. At least, it was less reliable than it had been. These were quiet implosions along an antiquated grid, systemic failures in giant dreamhomes that dotted the mountainsides of gated communities, plagued by the sounds of a dereliction of purpose... Poof! Poof! Poof! Poof!

They were confounded by the differences in anatomy. There might be too many differences between them to ever work it out... They were trying to communicate a lack of communication...in danger of being crushed under a weight of biology, slayed in a game of trivial pursuit. There is a love-song sung in a drone, propelled by beats that try to escape, tails from rockets that have hit their targets...and have no place to go, fuel spent on a singular mission, hormonal changes that used to serve a purpose, but now go to an ugly place.

A player on one side possesses a hegemony of the energy that the player on the other side needs to feel whole. The females can provide the males with the desired feminine energies. The males can provide the females with the desired masculine energies. Success for each is based upon the other players providing access to his or her energy.

It is an uncomfortable feeling, a splitting of necessities...a bifurcated reaction drowning a seed of balance. It is an odd combination where a substance is necessary, but its format is cumbersome. It is like casting breaths while fully clothed, immersed in a tank of liquid oxygen. Curiously, a dearth of the opposite energy on one end of the bell-curve could necessitate access to the other. It could be a scream for balance, underpinned by chemicals, where a short-term nexus can turn into a lifetime of mutual disinterest...where even the bridges are built through a division of labor. A rigid compartmentalization could mask the anguish... Ultimately, even the act of consummation could later be revealed as unsatisfying.

This dependency upon chemicals favors an obsession with lines of supply. A disruption in these lines would be a threat to access: A whole economy could be threatened. This supply would have to be ensured, and it would have to be promoted. Of course, an insecurity seeks to quiet that which reveals it: Its rites of commerce would have to be shouted and flaunted, like a person who extols a religion by wearing a shirt that says "god has been good to me!"

This lack of communication can be ameliorated through the use of devices; it is now the way that their most basic needs are met. The males usually sit in front of theirs, while the women are usually found with theirs attached to their ears. The males usually sit in private... There they can visualize and strategize the energies that provide them with access. Then, they might become mobile, arranging meetings where they can experience what they do not get a home. The women sit or walk in private, or in public...where they can discuss the energies that provide them with access. They might even group side-by-side—or step-by-step—while talking with someone else...emotionally experiencing what they do not get at home.

These energies are not always neat and orderly, however. There is an unconscious fluidity about them... Sometimes the signals are even mixed, inciting a fear that they might secretly be that which they had sought to demonize. This fear of being that which one does not want to be is a powerful force: It is the fear below the surface.

To be sure, any diversion from the traditional nuclear family risked rendering the sacred cycle obsolete. There was a suspicion of the ones who did not need this exchange. The men who desired the other men were especially despised because the acquisition of sex was so easy for them. The men who desired the women resented the fact that there was almost no commodification of sexuality for them: Gratification was easy. The women who desired the men were angry because they were not interested in purchasing their most sought-after commodity: The only thing worse than looking was not looking.

Still, there are unofficial ways in which to express disapproval, tacit actions to devalue their relationships. They would ask each other about their own husbands and wives, while they would not ask about the lovers—the non-legal equivalents—of the others. Frequently, they would not invite both of them to celebrations and ceremonies. If both of them were to go, they would not be expected to express open affection for each other. If they were to reference one in the presence of the other, they should refer to him or her as only a "friend". If both names were signed on a gift card, only one name might be acknowledged on its thank-you card.

This qualified intermingling contains a serious risk: familiarity breeds acceptance. In fact, a new apostasy is arising in fellow members of the opposite sexes who need each other's energies to feel whole: They are fulfilling their needs in ways that do not require the completion of the sacred cycle. This new expression of their needs does not even require a framework of political hegemony. They claim no insecurity when in the company of the non-procreative others; they mix with them freely. They even view their relationships as being equal to their own.

The laws and taboos would have to be enforced, covered by a shield of procreation, an escutcheon of privilege. Law enforcement officers were dispatched to sit on toilets in every region. There, they could force the issue. They could sit and wait, all day, arousing a curiosity in someone who just might be interested. They would be translators, too... It was suspected that this shadowy brotherhood used secret codes to communicate, but their codes had been cracked: a tapping sound was used to get another's attention; a motioning of the hand usually precipitated the next step; an acknowledgement of a yearning look in the eyes finally granted the illegal license.

These tactics of entrapment had brought unexpected rewards... In fact, many of these men had been caught sitting on these toilets with their pants down! Unfortunately, an inordinate number of these violators who were caught were the actual politicians and officials who authored the legislation which enabled the entrapment. Of course, they would have to leave office for this offense. There was another interesting wrinkle to all of this... The bell had been rung, and it was impossible to "unring" it, while out of all of the details, one of them really stuck out: They had given too much away to ever run for public office again. There was no more wiggle-room left on this slippery slope. It would be like giving the opposition a loaded gun, and allowing them to question these policies by piling on and on and on, drip, drip, drip...with no end in sight. That trigger had already been pulled, and there should be no taint on the party.

* *

He had already seen this fear on display, a gross representation. He had developed a love of painting at an early age, and he had become quite proficient. It was a medium where he could pursue a study of an early interest: the arranging of flowers. Earth loved to admire them, and she read into them nuances of support. He wanted to respect her by painting pictures of beautiful flowers... It would be like handing her a bouquet. He wanted to surround her with wishes of encouragement.

He had a special talent for making them pretty, but he added a strategic element. He arranged them in a special order, lending credence to her hunches. There was a meaning ascribed to each flower: A mood was associated with color; an intensity and nuance were ascribed to their height; their positioning and placement allowed for a tweaking of the syntax; the interaction of these qualities contained a semantics. It was a fusional synthetic morphology where each subtle difference could be read as a morpheme with a different meaning.

She was impressed with his prowess, and she grew to understand his messages. It was like a directory for twins...some kind of an innate ability, a dancing on a honeycomb, a language of the birds. She placed his works all over the walls of grottos and in the fields, on the shores of the oceans, from the flat land, inland, to the hills and mountains. It was her desire to read these messages in every climate, at different seasons.

One day, Night arrived, and went into a rage. She had seen the paintings and proclaimed them to be sex organs. She said that they were sex organs with an altered spatial dynamic. In fact, it was a representation of the type of aesthetic allegory that would lead to non-procreative energy exchanges. She removed these images, and replaced them with traditional ones of young males and females holding hands and looking into each other's eyes, while wearing clothing and bearing stances associated with his or her own sex, acceptable images of traditional heterosexuality, little icons of accepted normality.

• • •

Thank you, my Dears. Thank you. I seek from you an answer to the most important question of this age: Does the cream still rise to the top?

• • •

CHAPTER TEN

A lucidity of pieced-together cat-naps drifts to an aviary of sounds. A line of compression is reached where water provides percussion...accumulating in hanging receptacles, then purged through outlets with a sound of tapping on hollow wood. Here, old birds meet to execute rituals that they can no longer consummate. They stare at each other, making brittle contact with outstretched tongues and chicken skin in soiled, ruffled sheets. Then, they go to separate homes, in rooms like a cage, talk of each other and slowly forget the ties that hold the bond.

A familiar plea becomes tuneful as faint song grows stronger. An itinerant chorus patrols a hallway, singing of praise. It is an observance of another savior's birth. Thus, the apologia: He may not heal you, but he can give you strength. It is a march of the archetypes, a fawning assemblage, led by a leader of easy allegory and instinctive fear. He turns his head proudly to see into the rooms, looking for tears. An acknowledgement is made with a pleased expression, mistaking tears of the disappointment of such trite association for those of sentiment.

Jump out of the bed from a deep sleep. Lie back down. There is a discernible image, a bright ball abandoned in a pool of sludge. There are shifting bands of haze, advertisements in the sky: It is a celebration of the sale through beams in the clouds, security lights triggered after a home invasion. The natural resources are largely depleted. Urban heat islands rise like new mountain ranges with a shadow effect for arable land, adjoined by wires as neurological connections in the minds of sophists, searching for a way.

A card is lying on a table beside a bed in a hospital. At first, it looks like one of the standard stock, containing a wish for good health. It has been opened, however, triggering a recitation of a message. The voice is familiar, yet unique, like an outtake of a lost studio session. Still, it is garbled, as amplified through a loud-speaker and heard from a distance...down wind at a live performance.

In the shadow effect of the new mountain range

Where nothing will grow in the urban heat island

And concrete basin that traps the heat...

Then dries it out and blocks the rain

Stand monoliths of stone

Like epitaphs standing in a cactus garden

Of a time of surfeit, with sustaining fields flooded

Beyond their means and haphazardly placed

In a city in a forest of limited resources

A redaction of modernism that used to be bold

Geometries abstracted to promote a discourse

Find a hollow silence in a bleak environment

In a landscape of emotion without interaction

Posthumous recognition of a life-achievement award

Is found a corpse in brick-red clay

Where rose a phoenix to stretch its wings

In the dubious fame of a stolen phrase

A "new" empire state of questionable origin

Like standing in more than one shadow at once

An ersatz version of another's dream.

Another alarm sounds; an urgent message is received: The patient has experienced a qualitative change of condition. It is time for a shock therapy, an electric jolt, an artificial triggering of a perceived spiritual experience. Put on the hat and talk with the machine.

It is a pulmonary medicine without heart: It takes the breath away. A cat has climbed into the bed and sucked it out when no one was looking. A mask is affixed to portals of life. The air is thinning as reservoirs are drying. A hydraulic pump lifts paper-mâché arms as a punctual trickster administers a treatment. An irrigation system lies half-submerged in pillowy banks with remnants of moisture beading on the plastic web-rings.

* *

The emcee looks out into the telepathic fields, unseen and unheard, onto humanity. They are asking for another set of patriotic songs by burning candles, but, through his exhaustion and weight-conscious diet, the flashing lights reflect like brilliant ideas obscured by mundane questions, gasping like connections to a glorious past that they no longer feel worthy of receiving.

He bows to them with a mocked presumption that they appreciate his talents.

"Thank you, my Dears. Thank you. I seek from you an answer to the most important question of this age: Does the cream still rise to the top? It was my earliest goal to be an orator. I studied my subject to procure an impeccable grasp...to lay a firm foundation from which I could expound. Then, I delved into other subjects, both related and unrelated, so that my interpolations might have a sufficiently large sampling from which I could perceive patterns and strategies. I refused to proceed until I had matured, whereby I could pontificate upon the dilemmas of life, gleaned from having engaged its experiences. Thereby, I hoped to be capable of an understanding...to have reached a level of perspicacity necessary to procure a novel approach... or at least to be able to state it in my own voice.

I prepared my speeches and performances with an outline for clarity, and in a framework of gravitas. I dutifully practiced my delivery and elocution in a mirror, honing my craft with equipoise, smoothness and not a meager amount of subtlety. Soon, I discovered and uncovered a natural sense of timing. Still, just as I felt ready to make my debut, I realized that most of the audience was too gullible to address...an assemblage of implausibles, fueled by misunderstanding.

He bows to them again, as if for an encore.

"Well, I still love you, my Dears! I love each of you as my sugared adjurations...sweet mementos for my vanity presses. It is more material for my memoirs: Look for them someday... You may find yourselves in the chapter entitled, 'Mocked Offense or Outright Enjoyment?' There is certainly room available on the acknowledgements page...

"You are dear to me like the songs that I used to cherish...the ones around which I found myself clinging to juvenile emotion for wish-fulfillment. Of course, I realized that I was living vicariously through this intensity of the emotion of early-youth, so I boxed them up and threw them all away! It was one of the best decisions of my life...

A bulletin is announced across the monitors: A story of personal interest to all will be presented in an unprecedented manner of cooperation between the government and the private sector.

"Good morning! It is a bright and busy day at DIVINEAID. Let me introduce myself... I am Eris, the CEO, and I would like to take a few minutes to give you a tour of our new state-of-the-art facility... I think that you will be impressed. Our institution is fully accredited in a wide range of specialties... You might even notice some of our multi-disciplined professionals along the way, easily recognized by the matching colors of their job families. We have made it virtually impossible for you to confuse the level of status that each employee has reached. Remember, they are always available to assist you.

"This is the waiting area. Have a seat! You will notice that we do not have any chairs that recline: We do not want to encourage the family members of our patients to spend the night. Still, we offer a wide array of sugary drinks and sweet-and-salty foods in large portions for everyone to enjoy. Indulge! They are packaged in bright, colorful wrappers that might remind one of the colors of the tastiest and ripest fruits that are found in nature. Our marketing department has determined them to be evolutionarily patterned to appeal to these senses.

"Here, you can sit all day and listen to announcements which summon specialists to codes with cryptic names, denoting varying degrees of severity. The excitement can be so great that you might even have to stand and mill about... Then, you can play games with each other: You can wonder which codes might affect which patients. It is a kind of a death lottery...One of them might even affect one of your own.

"Come this way... I have something else to show you! Here we have the newly opened nurse's station. This modern unit features rooms with the latest high-tech gadgetry. Every room boasts the latest model of patient monitors. Sit in front of one and listen to the beautiful music! It can keep you busy for hours... These sounds are accompanied by an array of numbers, each monitoring the vital sounds of the patient: body temperature; pulse rate; blood pressure; and respiratory rate. It should also measure the level of oxygen saturation of the blood.

The monitor will beep if there is a problem... Of course, it could just be lending a false sense of security; or, it could have malfunctioned, providing us with an inaccurate reading. Still, it might not notify us at all... Thus, we are not responsible if we do not notice the warning signs of systemic failure: We cannot be in the room at all times. Besides, you just want us to tell you that your patient will be alright, and we can't do that. Remember, you can always push the 'call' button."

"This is Melpenome, how can I help you?"

"In addition, there are many tests at our disposal which aid us in diagnosing and treating a patient's illness. So many things could go wrong: infection; toxins that affect the nervous system; brain and spinal infection; damage to the blood vessels; hemorrhaging; autoimmune diseases...just to name a few. Of course, these sensitive tests require the expertise of our multi-disciplined professionals to conduct them and analyze them...requiring an impressive assortment of tools: needles; intense light; hammers; tuning forks; knives, etc.

"This is our most celebrated patient. Her condition is very grave. She has neurological issues, with attendant pulmonary distress. In addition, she is full of toxins and poisons, and now there is a clutter in her lungs. I've just received the results of her latest scan: It shows the signs of the development of an increasing area of infarction. Remember, just because there is no sign of bleeding does not mean that there is not any hemorrhaging...

First we will fit her with a mask. Next, she will be suctioned. Now is the time for another round of tests! We will subject her to a series of blasts of low-dosed radiation, neatly concentrated, and imprinted onto a plate. Then, it would be prudent to bombard her with radio waves and peculiarly strong magnetic fields so that we can see in deeper detail than the previous test. It is important to note that the water molecules of the tissues of our patients sometimes realign during this procedure! We could also attach electrodes to her head by needles or a special attaching agent. We will then expose her to different types of external stimuli such as drugs, noise, flashing lights, etc. Of course, we are always searching for some kind of brain damage, inflammation or disorder of metabolism...or even degeneration.

"Also, the issue of patient care is an incisive one, so we must remove and examine a small sample of tissue from the body...to study under the scanner. We will use a long thin needle to remove it, impaling the spinal sac, and removing some fluid. If we find that there is not a disorder in the neuromuscular system, we must still make sure that the patient doesn't carry a defective gene. Finally, we might decide to install rows of tubing through which we can inject a dye deep into the body. It is interesting to note that it might feel cool or warm as it circulates; it might even lend to one a metallic sensation.

"Still, the comfort of our patients is priority one... She will be safely ensconced during these testing procedures in a slab-like bed, and secured by high railings, which will keep her from falling out. If she were to protest and try to escape, we could call a code to designate this condition. Security would be summoned immediately! Of course, we could always bind her hands and her feet.

"The desire to escape is not uncommon in many of our patients, and any of a host of psychological maladies can befall her while she is in the hospital... thus, impairing her judgment. Anesthesia can take up to six months to fully leave her body. She might also experience extremely vivid morphine dreams. These dreams are often influenced by all of the poking, prodding and catheterizing that we do, sometimes instigating rather unpleasant and archetypal feelings of being bound and raped by numerous persons. In addition, there is a kind of psychosis which can affect persons who spend long periods of time in intensive care units. Of course, we have to focus on the more empirical patient issues... Emotional issues will only be considered if she were transferred to the mental health facility.

"Finally, the team of doctors will march into the patient's room at 6:00am, wake her from a deep sleep and ask her pertinent questions about her life. Then, they will assess her cognitive functions upon the clarity of her answers. Little attention will be paid to anything else that she will add, as they will have already formulated an original prognosis, and shall work hard to realize it.

"...How exciting! One of our most celebrated doctors is walking into the room. He is usually quite busy as the highly decorated head of our inpatient facilities, but he has taken a personal interest in our VIP...very important patient. In fact, he has just returned from the type of conference that trumps all others: doctor to doctor.

"Dr. Mors, would you like to make a statement to the loved-ones of the celebrated patient?"

"Her condition is stable, with no hope!"

• • •

Dear, it is true that this art is intrinsically tied to the vanity of personal appearance... I shall not deny it!

• • •

CHAPTER ELEVEN

The festival of humanity has become a mob scene. There is only one important question that remains unanswered: Did the victors actually slay the dragon, or was the dragon just not able to finish the job? It does not matter, Dear: They are celebrating a victory, and they have brought home the prize. Towns have been sacked... Exquisite works of art were removed from their cases and broken in fear... Bronze nude sculptures were scrapped and melted into weaponry.

"Women and children and the elderly are standing and cheering. Young men grunt and shout as they jump up-and-down in a huddle. The shining prize is lifted high into the air by the man with the greatest brute strength...who kisses it, and lifts his fist. Slowly, he parades down the middle of two lines of warriors, each taking his turn to touch it as it passes. Aging leaders of past victories extol them to enjoy this time...

"It is the greatest possible showcase for this culture, as the slickest of the gimmicks of their world will be on display as advertisements: They will have massive exposure. Large amounts of resources have been spent appealing to their lowest common denominators, like tourists who travel to once civilized lands—just to go shopping—or snicker at the nudity of their classical statuary.

"The greatest attention is paid to the art of the cursory presentation: fashion. Dear, it is true that this art is intrinsically tied to the vanity of personal appearance... I shall not deny it! Still, there is a relationship that it can form with a more complex art...suggesting it and enhancing it. Unfortunately, it is now primary...the perfect vehicle for this venue. In fact, it is so elevated that its subjects have become its slaves, expressing their reverence by carrying it—rather than wearing it—as they walk. Its utility has been completely removed.

"It is a fitting reward for a species whose best possible outcome is to die in its sleep. There is an obsolescence of organica... short-lived beings who derive their sustenance from the energy of others. It is where a hallmark of integrity is that one is merely trying to steal, rather than to kill. Soon, they will not have the energy to do either, as their cells will quit reduplicating...committing a type of suicide, an apoptosis. Of course, if they are cancerous, they can continue to divide to more effectively attack the host. Eventually, they might survive to an old age where they will face their most ironic brutality: The thing that they need the most—the touch of others—can be the most difficult thing to find. The fear associated with the appearance of obsolescence almost precludes it.

"It is a celebration of the predictable, an exuberance for the quotidian, captured in a performance piece where the musicians and dancers express their innate communication with their own cycles of life, presented as a universal experience. It is just about to start! Here are the players: the young women; the young men; the little girls; and, the little boys. The young men will attempt to court the young women... They are eager, but hesitant with a fear of access denied. The young women are aware of the desires of the young men and will try to lure them in ritual, and tease them with pomp. The little girls and the little boys will sheepishly imitate the actions of their role models, waiting for their turn. They are especially celebrated in an endearing way: They are the proof that this cycle of banality will continue.

"It is a play that is choreographed with percussive backgrounds. They are moving to a music as they act-out a ballet of a sexual division of labor. The young men are warriors, and they dance as if with spears and knives. The young women are maids, who dance as if with wash tubs and dirty clothes. There is a flirtation in this rigid compartmentalization, a relief in the knowledge of the role. It is a foreplay of selfishness, where the narrowest mind is acknowledged as the fittest for extending a gene-pool of undeserved entitlement.

"This is the sum of the predictable, tragic mathematics: The point of saturation beyond which a mixing and reconfiguring of the different cultures, perceived by five limited senses and experienced in truly novel ways, was now a cross-contamination..."

* *

A malaise descends as the implosions continue. A graphic is now being charted in a computer where the main artery is a branch with a limited destination. It marks, for the disinterested, the beginning of the end for their own adaptation. The shifting bands lift, and he catches a glimpse. Earth appears to him. The evolution of life has roughly mirrored the evolution of epistemology. Aesthetics was becoming more complex, as the puzzles of possibilities contained the seed. They were more than the sum of sunsets of representation: They were seeking more profundity, deeper possibilities...wider scope.

He sees the grottoes and valleys where his paintings used to hang. They are gone now...destroyed. The language that he spoke with Earth does not exist. A new language has been created: It is a language of expediency. Color and position still have meaning, however: Blue represents health hazards; red represents a danger of flammability; yellow warns of severe reactivity risks; white suggests special problems. Their positions on a sign denote their importance, as the numbers beside the colors signify the level of the risk: 4-3-2-1.

It is a culture with Sundowner's Syndrome, set to music that once embraced love and togetherness, but now touts thuggery, status, and the acquisition of items to be consumed. The pace of cultural change is portrayed as a cyclorama. The ones who craved authority purchased centers of entertainment... Limits were lifted on the monopolization of creative outlets, as individual voices were seldom heard. There were few, true luminaries...even fewer persons of letters. They had now becomes exotic in their own land, and left without a venue.

Myths are perpetuated in an impoverished land that is ruled by corruption... Food must be hoarded and stored for shortages. Currency is exchanged before it is useless. Disasters are exploited as a reason for looting. Telling the truth becomes a liability. There is an effortless duplicity in this culture of lying: They are indolent children who crave gods of discipline.

Another bulletin flashes across the monitors: A man covers his eye as he is interviewed in the aftermath of a storm. A tornado has ravaged his community, killing dozens of persons, splitting families. His house was destroyed around him, as he was picked-up in the funnel and spun around and around, blending thoroughly with dirt and debris. He is confused as to why he did not die with the others... He is deposited by the storm, but held in a fear of the unknown.

"He is a wonderful god!"

It is the oppression that is mystified the most...so pervasive that almost no one notices. It is inculcated into the everyday...slowly, until rationale is inured to a sense of universal justice. It answers a greeting by saying, "I am blessed." It is told of the horrific, but responds "god willing." Then, it denies this horrific by saying "god is good." Next, it will end this dialogue by saying "adios" or "godspeed." Eventually, it will putrefy...as this horrific is repeated in a pattern of justice, where what was once a suggestion of a reward for good deeds becomes the last defense of the dispossessed, "What goes around comes around." Finally, it succumbs to cynicism, "No good deed goes unpunished."

* *

"I'd like to announce a change of wardrobe..."

A head is lowered with a contrived vulnerability as each of his hands grabs the material from opposite sides, lifting it off of the ground. Next, one foot is placed behind the other as he bows his head and bends at the waist, and both legs lilt at the knees, outward.

"It was a present from a Bengali mystic, who retraced the paths of the ancient trade routes to secure, for me, the finest silk, available only in The Forbidden City in China. It seems that he wanted to prove his love to me through a romantic folly for our prospective romance, which had lasted exactly one night.

"He braved the windstorms of the Taklimakan Desert, in which he became lost, enduring the stifling heat of the day and numbing cold of the night, while bartering his fortunes with the nomadic descendents of Alexander's armies for the possession of the most fabulous gems that they had pilfered from the men that they had captured and forced to crawl under their jointly raised swords, desirous of impalement...and which he subsequently fastened onto the silk himself.

"The buttons were forged farther to the west in a Parsee's furnace, to which he navigated only by the positions of the fixed stars, whose map had been etched onto a weathered scroll during The Age of Aries in the Indus Valley, and recently rediscovered, via infrared technology...to which was added, days later, a delicate filigree, set by the hands of the most gorgeous young men of l'Arabie, on which were depicted the scenes of the exotic animals that frolic in their southern mountains, which surprise the imagination with thick forests of juniper.

"Finally, he charted a dhow across the Red Sea over errant waves caused by Eritrean pirates who pursued him all of the way, and over land, to the headwaters of the Blue Nile, where he secured a boat of papyrus, in which he sailed the extent of the great river to the great sea, only to pay a smuggler of black-market goods to accompany him—in avoidance of tariffs—to roughly retrace the path of Hannibal...over the straits of Hercules, up the Iberian coast, over the Pyrenees Mountains, across the Alps, and into my hands...just before showtime.

"I told him that a romantic quest for purity will only discover fanaticism. I wasn't going to wear it, but my other outfits had cocktail stains...

"Everything in my cup is fruit-based, and full of antioxidents.

"That fruit would be grapes, Dear...crushed and distilled beyond recognition.

"Still, I hope that you like it. The expense is mine, but the enjoyment is yours... Some of you are so beautiful, now that my drugs are kicking-in. Indulge me... It is such a strange irony that one must be narcissistic and self-absorbed to know oneself sufficiently to be capable of truly feeling the happiness and pain of another. Indeed, I can give you anything that you crave. We shall make sweet creampies for an insatiable universe! Shall it be an anonymous scene, blindfolded and on all-fours, with the door unlocked? Will it be stockings and heels or leather and caps? What? Don't be silly... I am always complimented! Besides, one should never blame another for trying. Ultimately, it is a pragmatic matter: If no one makes the first move, then nothing gets done. Now, don't make mama have to cut her switch! Oh, bringing culture to the masses can be so tiring...

"Put your hands together as part deux of our epic is racing toward you and screaming up the charts... It is called 'Theomania (The DIVA Affirmation)'"

An image appears out of the vaults. Semen and lipstick stains tug in a mucilaginous paste that obscures its clarity. White streaks cross its plane like loops in time, lost snippets of expressionism. A winged creature is seen emerging, testing its malleability as it flaps in black and white cloud banks of cigarette haze and mounts a pedestal of mother-of-pearl, raising its arms. A drum solo incites an erotic snarl and a flicking of the fingers, ecstatic reflexes of esoteric desires. It is the look of an anticipation of success, but from one who has already tasted it, and is returning to the table. It is an inherent knowledge of the goodness of satiety.

He jumps off the drum stand, flailing about through beams of obscure words from censored films, past, present, and future. It is a command of the spirit to the appeal of the archaic with the urgency of the moment...a classical setting with modern lines, a quest for voice in a study of emotional pitch and its influence upon language.

Breathy screams measure seismic evidence of tattered clothing and platform shoes. A tambourine shakes and slowly fades from a hallucinogenic fog of a delirium of postures in a timed sequence, as a drumbeat strikes every second...

The sound of a head banging against the ground
Shakes the flowers, and breaks the barriers
Releasing butterflies freed from the hothouse, united
Who indulge their dreams with perpetual reminders
Of impending success and contingent satisfaction
A nickhedonia embraced and in search of an audience
To question: What is the value of art
In a world where everything has already been created?

An aggregate of awareness in a time of youth
Imagined in a underpinning of fact
Self-styled creations, each with an autobiography in hand
With elitist tendencies and bohemian aspirations
Sprung from nothing but a knowledge
That an insular position is not a position of power
Spoken in a lingo from a ghetto of iconoclasts

Thus, offer themselves to an open discussion
In an open contempt for easy dichotomies
As the art of performance is natural for the artist
While concomitantly guarding the sanctity of hermitage

Then, define themselves in disdain for the answers

A reply of rejection in a restatement of the obvious

And a lack of concern for bellwethers and flocks

Who, sequentially, walk off of cliffs from vision impaired

So attached to being led that they pile-up at the bases, fawning

As the ones who believe in a spiritual realm

Where the perception of the senses is not

A measurable substance, but composed wholly of thought

In a formless motion, that may or may not be known

Except by an omniscient that holds all of the cards

In a power-play that has already been lost...

As their personal validation is based upon obedience

To their difficult task-master with this fixed result

But feel grateful for the terms of their self-renewing contract

When compared to the disciples of other faiths of discipline

Then rejoice in the realization of their humble insignificance

In this ritual celebration where they are branded for life

By the joy of receiving the punishment that they deserve

Or with a strict belief in a harmony with nature
Where a focusing of interest thereby focuses energy
Thus, every being is in a dialogue with the sacred
As the energy that one attracts equals that which is sent
Then, sit idly by in a universe without wisdom
Awaiting direction...to discover that they are self-consumed
In a cacophony of symbols and quantum puzzles
Like bodies traveling through another's penumbra
To reach the umbra in full eclipse
As each of the symbols only points to their end

Thus, seek refuge from superstition in an ecstatic
Denial of faith, and provide an uneasy audience
To another unquestioned, with the ones who believe
In a material base, in a reaction that is bound
Where the perception of the senses is concrete and fixed
With the certainty of knowledge of a measurable substance
Expanding, and more firmly grasped and perfectly gauged
With improving techniques of an outcome projected
In this refuge of the certain of theoretical perfection

While debunking ephemera in a literal distinct

But, amidst a curious respect for charisma's lure

And a fascination with the device of its orator's words

Irony emerges un-swayed by the draw of the magnetic poles;

Claim to knowledge complete is classed by philosophers in opposites

But the artist ascribes only one name to each: ideologues

And the nature of the ideologue is to view life in division

But works of art—like noble entreaty—are only made cheap

By a coercion of guilt, or an appeal to pity, thus...

A message is delivered from the artist to the critic:

There is only one thing that can be stated for certain:

Discovery of voice is not enhanced by a silencing of opinion;

Rather, it is discovered in the uncertain of the informed mystery.

Thus, defiance is declared in a statement of purpose

"To balance is sound, but to excel is divine!"

And deification is inferred in individual personages

As individual egos interact in a vast arena on canvas...

But explicitness is limited as two dimensions of painting

And a mandala of expression in a clipping of time

Or the emotional impact of a staged event of rhetoric

As the complexity of allegory requires a new medium

While the discomforted viewer can retreat to denial…

And as memories of stories contain fragments of history

The development of characters requires anecdotes of meaning

As a digression waits behind every exegesis

Where a depersonalization of one's own experiences

Allows a more integrated process of the personalization of fiction.

Hence, a purpose is attached to the question of value

And though the act of consummation is not ritual sacrifice

The dissolution of autobiography is the process of maturation

As compromise shall be made for the enhancement of plot

Though it shall never be allowed to compromise the message…

A heroine is leading the oppressed masses of a mechanized society from their overbearing lovers. There is a refuge in the beaux arts! There is an appeal in the arcane, a satisfaction in the recognition of the reference. A cup is raised from a gingerbread sleeve on a misty orange stage, containing substance. It is an offering to the crowd made in sequined boots for the self-obsessed, in the uncanny detail of one bristle of a brush.

And I am the messenger to an uncaring public

Of our knowledge in common that begs to be shouted

"We are the caretakers of the world without society's respect...

And there is more inspiration in one of our pin-pricks

Than in the endless volumes of your laws of containment!"

• • •

Look at us... Take a good look... We are the creators, the sustainers, the nurturers and the benefactors.

• • •

CHAPTER TWELVE

The years of pointless procreation had caused such devastation. The evolution of epistemology was shackled by exigency...the pursuit of refinement, tied to an economy. The spoils of empire provide a class of individuals with free time to seek its instruction and association. They possess the means to procure the materials needed to acquire it: conquest, education, training, understanding, creation and salvaging. Thus, its value is largely associated with the time spent for its procurement and acquisition: An association has been made between refinement and wealth.

Empire begins to crumble from corruption and over-extension. These are societies ruled by dynasties, where the seat of power is concentrated in a handful of families. Slowly, they convince an increasingly uninformed populace that they have a right to extensive, prolonged access to power. Interest and appreciation are replaced with arrogance. Bureaucracies of educators rule from cavernous rooms like petty dictators in plush chairs, arranged in an ellipsis. It is from this position where they vote to officially remove the lessons of history from the curriculum. In time, their students mature into adults who not only do not know these lessons, but cannot recognize their hallmarks. Eventually, they will not know the old version from the new version.

The restructuring has begun. It is said that a storm is coming, whose path is being tracked by knowledgeable persons: It will be a direct hit. When the smoke clears, everything will be different. Ocean is already encroaching upon islands... Warnings have been posted. If the surge is as bad as predicted, it will be certain death... Still, they do not leave... There is a bravery that is oblivious to intellect. There is a boldness without compassion. There is a blind willfulness in the face of another's conviction, presaged by a belief system that was codified in a similar mindset of survivalism.

A new economy is taking shape. The acquisition of basic necessities requires desperate measures. The price of heavy metals increases exponentially. The infrastructure laid in the days of glory is systematically cannibalized, halting public services. Copper and platinum are removed from machinery... Vehicles are rendered useless, and sold as scrap. Streets and avenues are riddled with missing pot-hole coverings. The aging underground system of piping is dug-up and dismantled as the disappearing supplies of potable water are finally left undeliverable.

The self-fulfilling prophecy has come full-circle. Here come the walking impugners, looking for someone to blame... They have issued a proclamation: The apocalypse is only for the unbelievers! The word has traveled at the speed of mass hysteria. The saviors can already be seen in the sky, for all eyes to see! This is the time! Here are the prophets, as scriptures have foretold. There is only one caveat: They are so beautiful that they cannot be seen directly. First, one must concentrate on their reputations—made great by a hindsight bias—concomitantly conveyed through an emotional assault on the rational processes; then, when one's eyes are completely closed, simply connect the dots along the different paths of intolerance...clustering illusions of threatening faces.

It is in such ruins where the signal is seen most clearly. It arises in the evolution, looking for acknowledgement, searching for others...seeking new parameters, waiting for acceptance. It flashes and flames; then, it is repressed and vanquished. It has sought its disguise as a paean to style, as a matter of necessity. It is found there, the sum of the greatest achievements of refinement, reaching their greatest numbers before the collapse; until, they are blamed for a dereliction which they did not cause. Finally, they are forced into margins, now relegated to style.

This is the cruel refuge of the unappreciated artist, forced from his or her natural home in the beaux arts, into the shadows of vanity and conceit. It is where a conviction of purpose and its right to access it, are forced into a servitude of its own oppression. It is here where the ostracized can go to personally distance themselves from their ostracizers, physically and tangibly, seeking an empowerment in the everyday. It is the servant who revels in the slovenly behavior of, or the unhygienic habits of, his or her employer. Of course, evolution is not inherently teleological: It has to be understood and made conscious; then, it can be guided.

* *

The desalinated haze opens to thin, insurgent needles in a ravaged land partially reclaimed. It is touted as an oasis of caring, an enclave of learning, a progressive bubble. A solution sprays into his nostrils, clearing his mind. He shakes his head, releasing tiny droplets like freed emotion that falls through the steam and flow as a wadi...into the sand, leaving a stain.

He continues past security, unseen in contemplation...a protective daze. He didn't know where he was going... He stepped off of the elevator, as persons in professional dress of color-coded uniforms passed by him. He turned to his left onto sanitized linoleum, toward a station of nurses who watch stark hallways with strained eyes...while talking softly under breaths as they examine patients' charts, located in neat compartments along the walls, outside the rooms.

It was like an autonomic function as he walked right into it, still unnoticed. He stopped and looked around: It was as he had seen it... The outstanding features were consistent; the details were incongruous. There was a single bed in the room. There was a bathroom to the left of the bed. There was a small table between them... There was a bouquet of flowers upon the table. There was a card lying next to the bouquet. There was what appeared to be an old lady with white hair lying next to the bed.

He recognized her immediately, as if through a disguise. It happened so quickly—all at once—in an elongated moment of mutual reverie where no records are kept and no evidence can be gathered...there was an emotional sinking, a sensation for fight or flight, then, a spike of elation: She could not be the one whom he had thought...she was too young to look so old.

Then, his vision expanded... The room was full of the industry of Death, and the industry of Starvation. Still, he was drawn to a presence that was made conspicuous by the absence of a moral core: Eris is sitting in a chair beside the bed. There is a smell from her breath of a putrefying protein that has sat for many days in the intestines of a carnivore, unmoved. Yet, her body seems wrapped in a fecal film...buttressed by the purposefully bared shoulder movements of a bully. Her face appears to be caught in a slow process of transmogrification into that of an angry marsupial, scouring a trafficked path for remnants of ones left indefensible by the ravages of time.

The lady is staring out of a window, as if searching for a familiar hand to touch her shoulder or lay a cool cloth upon her forehead. Her words are cluttered in conjured names of loved-ones past, and episodes of life's noteworthiness, interacting in a field that lies outside the room...privy to suggestion. Occasionally, an intelligible sentence is heard in the disjointed recollections...

Then, she sees his reflection in the window—an art-form too complex for two dimensions—and nervously raises a gnarled hand to him in acknowledgement...emotion searing through to a swaddled notion, blowing his cover...

"Thank you for the flowers!"

Eris leaps out of her chair, startled from her complacency of control.

"Stay down! Security! Stay down!"

A woman from the Management of Risk arrives almost immediately with two security guards who grab him by each arm, leading him away. The woman walks behind them as she organizes the required sets of paperwork that must be completed following every hospital incident. She hands him one set that he can complete: It is an official complaint form. Next she hands him one set that states that the hospital bears no responsibility for the cause of his possible complaint, and cannot be subject to associated legal actions of any kind.

"Please, come back!"

He can hear her voice as he is led away...

"I have something to say to you..."

This is the final stage for the cultural conduit in which the sacred cycle arose: the tribal mentality. It thrived in the organization of the tribe. It still permeated the structure of the kingdom. It persists into the nation-states. Still, it was evolving. Now, its system has formed a stem from which a culture of abandonment grows in the viscera of the trappings of the rewards of entitlement, reaching its most hollow representation at the end of this trepidatious path, a last gasp of the self-referential, a desperate reimagining.

This is where a new leader is inaugurated by an uninformed majority. Invoke the names from past eras! Return to the scene of past parades! It is a march of the appearance of tradition by the vessels of the original, human projections of procreation, two by two, male and female, officially arriving to celebrate the legacy of the sacred cycle on display as prizes won and brought home. Next, the codifiers, the lawyers in the judicial, and of course, the political branches, arrive at different times, each befitting the importance of his or her position. Then, the mystifiers of these laws, the ministers and priests, bestow their blessings upon this codification, and acknowledge them with a benediction.

The rewriting of history will proceed as scheduled in the cultural apotheosis of the new union of necessity, the new tribe. It is a formula of a bifurcation fused, a synthesis envisioned as pristine and preindustrial to evoke a sense of continuity. A god had been replaced with a goddess, whose consent would be sought in matters of morality. The men would remain the primary leaders and the greatest warriors, though the women would have access to these roles, and show remarkable abilities. The women, however, would be the sole conduits of this deity... the Shaman of the tribe, the keepers of the ancient wisdom.

It was a romantic epic. There were the action scenes for the men. There were the personal stories for the women. There would be a war with the non-procreative forces, with a great and decisive battle. The men and women would join as one to save their tribe from these non-procreative forces, who would be determined and treacherous, and inflict many casualties. Still, just as it seems as if the enemy will win, they pray, as a tribe, on the cycles of life, to the goddess for a miracle...and the miracle is granted. Amazingly, all of nature begins to defend procreation. The deity itself begins to erupt to rid itself of its scourge, invoking the aid of the guardians of tradition —the mentors of the sacred cycle—in this final victory.

This new history is filtered and disseminated exclusively by the talk-show, as news and entertainment renew their vows with this common interest in a common enemy. Now, every story that is released to the public will have to be parlayed across this national coffee table. Here, the hosts sit high above the masses, shielded from important, ground-breaking events by vanity lights, a lack of real knowledge and personal animosities.

They are discussing a subtext to the celebration, the activities of Minerva. Her work is under investigation: She has attracted their suspicion. She does not look quite like they look. She does not sound much like they sound. She bears the characteristics of uniqueness: She must be disingenuous. She has gone further than they thought possible. In fact, her views are an apostasy. She has questioned the moral fabric...the moral right. She has questioned the sense of entitlement. It is upsetting to them.

The blotched face is being interviewed by the hosts, and he is ready to explode. He wants her to be arrested and questioned. She should be charged with treason. She should be held at a detainment center, at an undisclosed location—removed from scrutiny—where probable cause is simply one's presence. Of course, if it is thought that she might have collaborators, then she should be tortured to surrender their names.

The hosts agree with the blotched face. They say that the tactics of interrogation are unfortunate... Still, the children have been protected. The country has been protected... There has not been another major attack since the last one. It is obvious that this policy of containment works: There are now volumes of unsubstantiated material to prove their point. Besides, they will only inflict the stimuli to the point of confession...

A news bulletin flashes across the monitor: A murderous villain has been killed, associated with horrific crimes against Empire and its citizenry. Spontaneously, a crowd of exuberant young men and women gather in front of the facades of buildings which embody the days of glory. These are the young persons who were reared listening to the recollections of these bygone days, while personally enduring the bleak reality of decline, of diminishing expectation. They are desperate for a renascence of the power and authority invested in Empire: They want their inheritance.

It is the historical continuum of societal enervation. It is the allure of the chimera for the generation that will have to learn that it cannot be sustained by myth. The young men wave their fists in the air, amidst nationalistic banners.The young women join them in songs that tout the only fields of triumph that they know: the fields of sports. Curiously, their favorite anthem is one that has been corrupted from its original intent of glorifying personal triumph, to that of the tribe.

Now it is time to cheer the reassertion of the energies of the sacred cycle. The young women climb to the tops of the young mens' shoulders, waving their fists with encouragement. The young men eagerly assume the position of the infrastructure, the means; the young women eagerly assume the position of the consumer, the beneficiaries, as their hands and fists wave in the air toward the heavens...in anticipation of the recapture of the riches of Empire past, an imperfect diagram of the sacred cycle in pyramidal effigy.

The stories of the villain's capture are immediately spread by the government and its ancillary services, flooding and skewering the public's belief with the importance of the first impression. An overiding version is stressed to silence any rational opposition to the agents of ownership and control: The villain's capture was only made possible through the use of enhanced interrogation practices, or torture. This is the version of the story that is the necessary proof to ensure that the safety and prosperity of the new tribe will not be subject to codes of conduct and ethical standards.

One thing is clear: The forces of the enemy are everywhere. They are in every race, ethnic group and sex. It is time to rebuild the firewall... This is the place of subterfuge where one can go to seek time to delay a clear proclivity of direction that one does not like. It is a last refuge—a place of self-proclaimed victimization. There, it searches for any possibilities...any contrived evidence, to continue a belief in the face of evidence to the contrary. It is emotional privation. It is proclaimed naivety. It is a monster who gladly devours its own tail to conceal a question that changes a paradigm.

* *

He returns to the hospital. A security man notices him as he arrives, charging the air with a zeitgeist of redoubt. He increases his pace to the elevator as urgent queries, like electric july-flies in imaginary tree-tops, search for responses and locations. This is not a drill. He exits the elevator as a code is blaring overhead in a phrase announced twice, repeated every 20 seconds. He can see the nurse's station as scornful sets of eyes zig-zag the hallway in a pretense of care. He turns the last corner to her room as the security men approach from the opposite direction. He grabs the door and opens it, but the room is empty.

The woman from The Management of Risk has joined security, reinforced by a team of code-responders. He looks down, eyes drawn along a forlorn path of fallen petals to a waste basket. There, on top of the pile, is the bouquet of flowers that had been on the table, untended and discarded as empty affection. It seemed grossly inappropriate, a withering connection to a fading recollection, wilting flowers in a desiccated landscape. Then, something shifted in the pile. It was extremely slight, like the imprint of a mime's hand upon a surface defined only through the deductions of consciousness. Still, it moved again. He moved closer...shifting a weight upon an unnoticed tipping-point, a feathery final straw of a force of will. There was the sound of something...a fluttering of wings around a gurgling of honey, a marketplace whose purpose was a bartering of joy. It refocused his mindset... Something was in it—remnants of syntax—a repeating of a refrain, familiar song fragments. It sang of innocent joys and painted sky beneath a rustic camp with handsome young men exploring their urges in teepees and tents, constructed for coddling...a nursery rhyme wrapped in an endearment of words, an assault on insensitivity by angry wordsmiths.

A gentle whisper brushed his face, a signal on an afflatus...an extolment to follow the song. He began to be transformed... There was a hum, the sound of a cello. Trade winds blew in a low-pitch, a slothful vibrato in a child-like refrain to a movement whose path is intrinsically shielded from disillusionment. It followed a rhythm that was steady, but gradually revealed an increasing tension. He felt a massaging current, a sweet effleurage, guiding him to look to the sky, weight applied to strings, melting impasses...

He soared over the Atlas Mountains...across the ocean stream, as songbirds still sing. They fly en masse, but separate periodically, reassembling like flakes of graffiti left by ancient lovers, dispersed by the winds and re-deposited. They guide him to this mountain of rock, arising from this bath. Bow strikes strings to a lively dance, a spiccato, an inclusionary circle. They swirl and sing in a spiraling ascent, cumulative experiences in a long-term quest.

Prometheus is waiting under a circle of trees...looking for answers, spread-out and compartmentalized, trying to concentrate on a framework and passageways, superimposing what he really wanted onto what he really had. Something was still missing from his experiences with females... He wondered if it were what the other males had done... There was an emptiness. He had fulfilled the sacred cycle, but he was left unfulfilled. He was lying there in frustration, waiting for a deliverance.

It was the smell of his neck, the pressing of his touch. It was as it had always been... It had maintained its beauty. A curiosity had become a necessity. What had been the apparent had become the obvious as they looked upon each other: There was a deeper way to consecrate their bond! The made a bed in the dirt. They noticed rocks, gathered into piles. What was once a shelter was now a historical marker. What was once called profane was a door to the sacred.

Prometheus was more active in the beginning and more passive in the end. He, himself, was more passive in the beginning and more active in the end. There was a sensation to the nipple. There was an exploration of the spheres. There was a rumbling on the ground from an entanglement of feet. There was a bright string bowed closer to a bridge, a *sul ponticello*, resplendent.

All of nature was smiling. The lovebirds were nesting. The lambs were milking. The pups were suckling. The ants were working. They continued as always... None of it mattered now, however: They had a different agenda, a different purpose. It was proclaimed with every thrust.

"goodness!"

"GOODness!"

"GOODNESS!"

There was a love of a strategy in the shape of a form, a visual cue. Then, an expectant contraction, a withdrawing of surf, a grinding, a pounding, a tickling, a caressing. It was synergistic and mutually beneficial, a deeper voice in a tight embrace...gushing fuel, self-cleansing and renewable. A tidal surge roared onto a rugged shore, as golden ripples slowly flooded as honey into veins, down to the toes, filling-up and lingering with a feeling of completion, dripping off of folds stretched outward by hands, opened-up all of the way with the creaking of a melon, and onto the ground.

He pressed closely to Prometheus as his vessel overflowed with his presence inside, grinding onto a fixed point, to the end of his shaft. Slowly, their momentum moved in a circular path as he took the shaft of Prometheus and readied it, like an ear of corn oiled by two bare hands, cupping it to disperse the liquor of its broth... and nuancing its head with his fingertips while teasing the lip of its crown, around and around in a resonance of their bodies – honed in a frequency of movements – like the reverberations of a Tibetan singing bowl...this balance of the masculine and the feminine in one body, augmented by another, from the personal to the greater to the universal, producing the sound of this inextinguishable breath...deconstructed and reassembled like a conflation of a déjà vu: "quiet, where need is...and talking to the point..."

Message received! A mutual recognition had a truth to tell: It was an epistemological apotheosis of the male tendency. It was a natural avant-garde. Their love was biological, but it was not based upon an imperative, a call to procreate. Their love heeded a different call...that of a need to experience. In fact, it was a natural deviation of the need to experience.

Still, it was more. Experiences were not enough... It required a critique of them, a cultivation of sophistication. It craved a union, but valued the individual. It was enhanced by a pursuit of voice, a development of taste. Everywhere it sought the process of refinement. It enriched the fuel, and reinvigorated the passion. It sought a diversity of experience, but with an appreciation of its quality.

It was not violent. It sought no legalized ostracism or oppression. It was not innately threatened by the other forms: There were proclivities of energies, but there was no hegemony. Each player possesses enough of the opposite energy to preclude it. A player on one side can facilitate the player on the other sides' realizing either of the energies involved, in varying combinations and degrees, at one time, or at the same time, if desired.

They could experience the more male-associated types of satisfaction that are born of penetrating. Yet, they could experience the more female-associated types of satisfaction that are born of being penetrated. They had a need for both of these experiences, but they needed other males to complete the cycle. Interestingly, they had enough of their own female energy in the consciousness to preclude their needing to be supplied: There is a DIVA behind every curtain.

It was a new direction. It was not a replication of a more prevalent cycle. They needed no artificial devices to complete the cycle. Its emotional needs were in accordance with its physical components. Nature had even equipped them with delightful means to achieve this balance. It provided them with a special organ that lay inside of their inner sanctum, at just the distance of the average size of a penis...waiting there to be discovered, miraculously.

* *

A snipping sound is heard as a ribbon is cut, christening the alternative stage on Earth... igniting a scream at the pulpit of the predictable voyeurism from the auspices of morality. They have hurt her with their openness. They are killing her with their visibility. Their acceptance of themselves has impeded her locomotion. She drags her body along the periphery of the firewall, an amphibian too long on land, facing an incline on a hot, dry road. Sporadic squeals of terror chart a journey marked by the grunting noises of slowing motions of helplessness, high ridges of reassurance of positions of victimization...nails in the dirt, now forcibly bent...sprawling as the arms of a succulent—filled with emotion—whose meager validation is stored in every trunk...a broken vial of pain awakened from an anesthetic, unable to speak clearly.

"I them...

"I THEM...

"I saw...

"I SAW THEM.........

"AND...........

"THEY CAN LOOK EACH OTHER IN THE EYES!"

Hands curl as if arthritis has seized her, robbing her of her youth, precluding personal industry. She cannot use them now: They are good for nothing. She has seen something that she cannot explain. She rocks back and forth, shaking her head, mumbling to herself in a fetal position…a balled up child resentful of being birthed in a universe that she cannot control.

She cannot drag her body another inch. She will have to have assistance. She will have to have complicity. There is one last tactic, one last ploy: Appeal to the most indefinable fear…the psychological underpinning in the bulk of the mythos of this procreation. She imagines a wound, to focus on a scar…helpless imagery of the old and infirm in a second childhood of possibility of revisiting a separation anxiety in a hospice of hurt, collapsed but still proselytizing…finally resembling a sign of peace, broken and reattached as a sign of a desperate, disappearing faith.

"WHO WILL TAKE CARE OF YOU WHEN YOU ARE OLD?

"WHO WILL TAKE CARE OF YOU WHEN YOU ARE OLD?

"WHO Will take care of you when you are old?

"Who will take…care of…of…"

Empire is crumbling. Everything is collapsing. The environment is changing as the stasis has ended. The social cataclysm has exposed the limitations of the old values of adaptation. The tribal mentality that buttressed the primal emotions is now a codependent parent to its spawn of incompetent family. Simultaneously, a new technology is introduced, engaging the advantageous variation. A graphic is being charted where an extant artery expands into a branch with an unlimited destination. It establishes for the interested a new phase of their own adaptation.

The signal is getting stronger. It can now be transmitted and received anywhere. In addition, the furtive years of tolerance won have helped to create a consciousness of expectation. This convergence has triggered a movement, conscious of a purpose. Biology is the catalyst, transforming a conversation: Aesthetics is infused with substance. Somehow, they are ideally suited to access this new world... They have engaged each other in the new technology. They are talking in its forums. They are finding their brothers and sisters all over the world. Suddenly, the graphic comes to a halt in a jam of information...interwoven possibilities, blocked by an antipodal necessity. Mathematics will no longer support an exclusive epistemological expansion in the old direction. Still, it is unknown if the new direction will supplant the old, or become its complimentary coefficient. In any event, a choice will have to be made... This is the place where greater technology and increased population will require a decision to embrace the new direction or destroy it.

The winged creature emerges from outside the ledger lines of time-loop, highlighted amongst the stars by a flashing spotlight. Acoustic strings change the perception of its tone and distance with the striking of each note, exposing fragments of cryptic verse upon patterns of air like embroidery that flaps with a movement unknown, revealing words, things, ideas and persons, discovered in the abrogation of a truth attached to its own hermeneutics, the revelation of a shared breath.

As species mingled in the seas to cultivate survival won

In awkward gait transitioned to a firmer foot to stage the hunt

For scraps of meat upon the ground where instinct cries of animal urge

Whose meaning is betrayed by man in tongues of tied expedience

Thus, man creates these gods divine to file and claim inheritance lost

And frames a view in narrow sight as a spiritual ideologue:

With sun and moon as man and woman in their celestial reflection

To legitimize this union framed to an entitlement of lineage
As sun restricts nutrition starved for the reverence of his attention

And moon remains in shadows soft, conceit covert with vanity

Who rise and fall but only touch in a parallax of movement

The figments of a trompe l'oeil in a spectacle of arrogance

But concepts float upon the breath in visions of a deeper race

Emerging from the discord of this fractious union apparent made

As buds deprived of sun and shade find deeper roots in richer soil

While nourishèd in self-respect these blossoms form within the thorns

With knowledge that is held entwined, sequestered with derisive names

Like pretty petals pulled-apart from wishes asked of others' pain

In syntax of a purpose joined to celebrate pursuit's unique

To propagate this language known outside the thorns of vulgar's reach

In perfumed gardens yearning for these fragrant blooms of finer art

A validity of the genuine grows out of its necessity of artifice

From its self-fulfilling prophecy in a mythos of a chance occurrence

Reveals: the apotheosis of refinement from its burden of necessity.

"It is the most painful elitism to accept, Dears...the elitism of the obvious. It shares one thing in common with slander: It only is...if it isn't true.

"...And so it has come to this... The old amusement park is scheduled to close, but will remain open indefinitely into a leveraged future. Here they come...like pilgrims descending upon one of their shrines, now dressed in biblical garbs to conjure their messiahs, as pages in a children's book. Peddlers and hawkers have packed their trailers full of commemorative wares... Ferris wheels rise over palm trees ringed and trapped in encasements of white concrete, halting further growth. Legs dangle from buckets in the sky, as disagreements are heard among persons who do not want to sit together.

"A group of young men and young women have assembled to play a game. The young men sit side-by-side, as the one at the end of the line takes his hand and slaps his face, bowing his head in the direction of the next young man...as his head bows in a domino effect to the end of the line...where the action is reversed, and repeated, like a row of metal balls suspended from strings in a model of classical inertia...as the young women stand across from them and giggle, while discussing which ones are the cutest.

"A middle-aged man and woman encourage their son and daughter to board a ride that they used to enjoy, as did their parents. It is located in a centrifugal arena with cars that move over facsimiles of bumps-in-the-road, and other impasses...on a track lined with mawkish paintings of an idealized community, with pictures of houses and streets and mountains and valleys. They sit on a bench and watch as their children are locked-in, and the ride begins. Slowly, it cranks and chortles as it begins to traverse the obstacles... Then, a voice from a loudspeaker exhorts, "Do you want to go faster?" The children look at their parents, who nod approvingly, and join their peers and their parents in the consensus... "Yes! Yes!" This exhortation and response are repeated several times, as no one ever seems to realize or care that the voice is a recorded prop.

* *

It is a hot, June day as the volunteers are busy with preparations. The little genius cups his hand to his ear and runs down a series of steps onto the pavement, and to the end of the grand boulevard to gain a full view of its main tributaries. Hurriedly, he removes it to the top of his forehead, creating a shield to increase his vision. Then, he jumps back—to face the boulevard—and pulls a scarf from his trousers. It waves in the air with the colors of the spectrum, the enveloping borealis—a flag without borders—moving in the pulsing airwaves that ricochet through the building.

"There are millions and MILLIONS of us!"

...And it is lead by a Lesbian. They come on foot, on wing, on skates, via stilts, atop floats, on fire trucks, inside convertibles and by antique cars. Throngs of family welcome them from the sidewalks, from the roofs, the street-cafes, on the balconies and in the windows. It is not like a meeting; it is like a reunion. Here are the faeries, the dykes, the drag-queens, the trans-persons, the bisexuals and the butches. Here is a burgeoning, applauding support of the straights who are not narrow. They sing and shout and dance until day turns into night and a cool breeze blows upon this midnight cabaret. Here gathers the diaspora, uniting the totems from across the world, revealing themselves from behind the masks. A scepter is raised high above the crowd.

"Look at us… Take a good look… We are the creators, the sustainers, the nurturers and the benefactors. We give to society and society's children, though they are rarely of our blood. We are the caretakers of the world without society's respect… You can arrest us. You can torment us. You can prosecute us. You can even kill us. Still, we are not afraid…not anymore. Our realization was born in an imperative: If you kill the caretakers, the patient will die.

Ten slender fingers slip into white dinner gloves in stark illumination with face and neckline against an opaque background. Eyes close and arms begin to sway…slowly at first, finding expression in exhilaration, rocking and bouncing, fluttering as from wing, feather and cape to translate into words what was signaled from its furtive stirrings:

"This stage is ours, Dears!"

A sweeping trajectory is traced from waist to head, where, with a flick-of-the-wrist, a snap…and lights.

"Make it magnificent!"

The heavens explode along a north-south trajectory of shoreline like a breach of helium, releasing enthralled voices of kindred spirits of shooting stars with fiery petals, proclaiming their freedom. Struck in its own realization, DIVA lights upon a dais about its festive, reunited diaspora, as one leg lifts ninety degrees with a wiggling abandon. Arms lift slowly and climb to extend high above the face, as wrists flex and hands cup outward as a numinous mast for a shimmering gauze, cascading in the breeze.

• • •

This stage is ours, Dears!

• • •

OTHER HELPFUL BOOKS BY *CHARLES L. WHITFIELD, M.D.*

A Personal Workbook and Guide to the Best-Selling *Healing the Child Within*

In this book Dr. Whitfield continues and expands the ways to heal our Child Within which he began to describe in his best-selling Healing the Child Within. He presents specific guidelines and exercises for getting free of the chains of co-dependence and having grown up in a dysfunctional family.

HCI Book Review

A Gift To Myself

Charles L. Whitfield, M.D.

The National Best-Seller!

"A concise, comprehensive and rather remarkable integration of the theory and practice of healing the child within; we highly recommend this useful book."

Herbert L. Gravitz, Ph.D.
Julie Bowden, MFCC

OTHER HELPFUL BOOKS BY CHARLES L. WHITFIELD, M.D.

Depression hurts. Sometimes it overwhelms. But what do we really know about it? Is the current opinion about its nature and treatment true? Whether you or someone you know suffers from depression, you have choices that will enhance recovery. Rather than relying on the drugs-alone approach, which is expensive, often toxic, and doesn't work well, there may be other more effective and less bothersome recovery aids.

Renowned physician, psychotherapist and best-selling author Charles Whitfield *offers new hope.*

CHOICES FOR HEALING

CHARLES L. WHITFIELD, M.D.

THE TRUTH about MENTAL ILLNESS

CHOICES FOR HEALING

CHARLES L. WHITFIELD, M.D.

One in five American adults suffers from some kind of "mental disorder." The Truth about Mental Illness uncovers the myths and realities of disorders such as post-traumatic stress, ADD, anxiety, eating disorders, drug addiction, schizophrenia and personality disorders. Whitfield offers cutting-edge research into their causes; why the real causes are often overlooked; how clinicians and patients can avoid misdiagnosis and how to prevent bothersome and sometimes dangerous drug effects.

HCI Book Review

OTHER HELPFUL BOOKS BY *THE WHITFIELDS*

This book is a continuation of Volume I, Choosing God: A Bird's Eye View of A Course in Miracles -- of this two volume pair.

In this book I pick up where the first book ended. Here I summarize 15 more key Course topics plus a new original chapter, The Universal Message of the Course in which I compare the Course to world religions and spiritual paths, including Alcoholics Anonymous and other Twelve Step Fellowships.

"Charles takes us into the heart and soul of A Course in Miracles"

Jyoti and Russell Park, PhD
Center for Sacred Studies

Teachers of God

Further Reflections on
A Course in Miracles

Charles L. Whitfield, MD
Author of Healing The Child Within
and
The Power of Humility

mhp
muse house press

"Spiritual Awakenings breaks new ground both for Barbara Harris Whitfield and for the field of near-death studies."

Bruce Greyson, M.D.,
Chester F. Carlson Professor of Psychiatry and Neurobehavioral Sciences, University of Virginia School of Medicine

OTHER HELPFUL BOOKS BY *THE WHITFIELDS*

While summarizing the main messages of A Course in Miracles with remarkable clarity, in this new book Charles Whitfield goes well beyond the other books on the Course.

Here the best-selling author of *Healing the Child Within* and nine other self-help and recovery oriented books, draws upon his vast clinical experience assisting people with addictions, "mental illnesses," and other problems in living.

"In this book I give you a reader friendly summary of what I and selected other writers believe to be the most important spiritual psychology in the *Course*."

In my over 30 years assisting countless people with a variety of mental, emotional, behavioral and relationship problems, I have come to realize that many of them have been misdiagnosed and mistreated. In fact, most of them were not mentally ill.

In my book, You May Not Be Mentally Ill I share research and experience and offer hope and another way that may successfully address what may not be a "mental illness."

Charles L. Whitfield, MD

OTHER HELPFUL BOOKS BY *THE WHITFIELDS*

Remembering what happened in any traumatic experience is basic and crucial to healing. The memory of abuse survivors has been questioned and challenged by all sorts of people, ranging from perpetrators to family members. More recently, this memory has been challenged by a combination of accused family members, their lawyers and a few academics who claim the existence of a *"false memory syndrome."*

Charles Whitfield, M.D., brings his clinical experience and knowledge about traumatic memory to examine, explore and clarify this crucial issue.

"So much has been written and said about the soul. In this book, we are shown the soul. Whitfield illustrated how to live from our soul and relate to the souls of others.

I have come to regard this book as a postcard from Whitfield's soul to ours, and my advice is to read it, say "thank you," and put it into practice."

Bruce Greyson, M.D.,
Chester F. Carlson Professor of Psychiatry and Neurobehavioral Sciences, University of Virginia School of Medicine

www.ingramcontent.com/pod-product-compliance
Ingram Content Group UK Ltd.
Pitfield, Milton Keynes, MK11 3LW, UK
UKHW041829200726
13854UKWH00002BA/897

9 781935 827030